THE GUN OWNER'S HANDBOOK

THE GUN OWNER'S HANDBOOK

A Complete Guide to Maintaining and Repairing
Your Firearms—in the Field or at Your Workbench

LARRY LYONS

The Lyons Press
Guilford, Connecticut
An imprint of The Globe Pequot Press

The Lyons Press is an imprint of The Globe Pequot Press.

Printed in the United States of America

10 9 8 7 6

Library of Congress Cataloging-in-Publication Data

Lyons, Larry.
  The gun owner's handbook : a complete guide to maintaining and repairing your firearms—in the field or at your workbench / Larry Lyons.
      p. cm.
  Includes index.
978–1-592-28742-0
  1. Firearms—Maintenance and repair—Handbooks, manuals, etc. I. Title.
TS535.4.L96 2006
683.4´03—dc22

                                                    2005028283

CONTENTS

CONTENTS

INTRODUCTION

When the editor approached me about doing a comprehensive, "one-book-does-it-all" guide on the cleaning and maintenance of sporting arms I first thought he was on the far end of a long martini lunch. It seemed like there's been enough how-to this and how-to that written about guns to fill the Lincoln Library. "Yeah, but not all in one book," he countered. "It's mostly just dibs and dabs scattered about in manuals and magazine articles spanning decades. Just give it some thought." I nosed around a bit and he was right. I didn't find a single book guiding the average firearm owner through day to day life with his guns, keeping them all well and happy. Further discussion brought up more ideas, such as caring for all the stuff that goes along with guns, like scopes, slings, holsters, and cases. They're important, too. And why not throw in troubleshooting and the common repairs we can do ourselves to save a few bucks? And we must go into emergency repairs when far afield, too. Of course, plenty of useful general fiream knowledge will surface in the process. Thus the project was born. My goal from the beginning was to make this book useful to everyone. It includes all the basics for the newcomer just discovering the magical world of shooting, yet is comprehensive enough to teach even the saltiest dogs new tricks.

Today's shooter has a vast array of products at his disposal that make gun care easier and better than could have been dreamed of just a decade or two ago. Ironically, this plethora of stuff also leaves all but the most knowledgeable of shooters in total confusion. Couple this with a multitude of misconceptions and myths both new and old, outlandish product claims, and more different types of guns on the shelves than you can shake a cleaning rod at, and it's no wonder gun care now seems like some form of voodoo magic.

This book puts the gun owner's feet firmly on the ground, sorting the wheat from the chafe, if you will. Of course, it would be impossible to detail every bottle of chemical, every gadget, widget, and gizmo that comes and goes from dealer's shelves, but there's really no need for that, anyway. What brand name is on a given item seldom matters. All one really needs to know is the proper procedures of firearm care and what types of chemicals and tools best accomplish it. This, and perhaps the owner's manual or disassembly guide for your particular gun, is all you will need to keep all your sporting guns in top working order. I will readily admit, though, that I did not have the ambition to delve into modern military-type arms. Perhaps another day.

By way of credentials, I was born and raised in Dowagiac, Michigan, home of the famous Niedner Rifle Company which was widely renowned during the heyday of the custom rifle. I scurried around under the feet of master craftsmen trained by A.O. Niedner and soaked up the knowledge of Tom Shelhamer, world-class stockmaker and general manager of the Niedner Company. I built my first custom rifle at the age of thirteen. When I was nineteen I started a wholesale gunstock business. I've been a licensed gunsmith since the day I became old enough to get a license thirty-five years ago. I've hunted from the Arctic to Africa for most everything there is to hunt and haven't embarrassed myself too badly in competition shotgun shooting. While a game warden in the Pacific Northwest I was a law-enforcement shooting instructor, teaching combat shooting with both handgun and long gun to multi-agency officers as well as training other instructors.

From the writing perspective, for a number of years I wrote a monthly gunsmithing column for *Guns & Ammo* magazine and another on general firearms for *Michigan Out-of-Doors* magazine as well as feature articles for publications such as *Outdoor Life*, *Muzzle Blast*, and *Muzzle Loader*. If you hang around guns long enough you're bound to learn something and I reckon by now I must have some sort of degree from the school of hard knocks. Now I pass it on to you.

Chapter 1

PREPAREDNESS PRECLUDES PROCRASTINATION: THE WORK AREA AND TOOL ORGANIZATION

There are probably folks out there who consider gun cleaning one of life's great pleasures, but I've never met one. We all love to shoot, but cleaning up the mess afterwards ranks right in there with snaking out a clogged toilet drain. In the old days when corrosive ammunition could eat into a gun in a matter of hours it was a given that upon returning home from a shooting session, first and foremost the gun was cleaned. With today's benign ammo that worthy creed has fallen by the wayside. Now we look for some excuse to put it off. The fact is, the sooner the gun is cleaned after shooting the easier it is to remove fouling. Also, once the act of procrastination begins the more inclined we are to keep it going. What started as "I'll do it after dinner," turns into

"I'll do it tomorrow," which then goes to "as soon as I get a chance," and ultimately ends up leaving your thought process entirely. Leaving the bore uncleaned and the outer metal unprotected for a day or two may be harmless but each passing day is further invitation for rust to rear its ugly head. The more organized and better equipped we are the less the temptation to put the chore off.

WORK AREA

Trying to clean your gun on the kitchen counter while the little lady is cooking dinner is not good. The dining room table isn't so swell either. Having your own, user-friendly work area with all the necessary gear at hand greatly minimizes the temptation to procrastinate. It also takes much of the curse off cleaning chores.

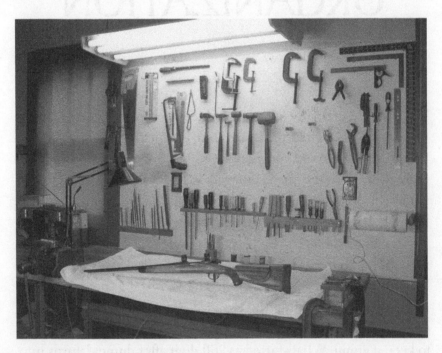

A clean, well-organized work area helps prevent putting off gun cleaning chores.

The area need not be a full-blown workshop but it should be well lit and have some sort of ventilation such as a window or outside door. Many of the chemicals used in firearm care are somewhat odiferous, a few are down right obnoxious, and some can even pose health hazards when inhaled in excess.

THE BENCH

We obviously need some sort of bench. It need not be fancy but must be stout, the sturdier the better, to keep from tipping bottles over and dumping guns on the floor. It should also be large enough to accommodate full-scale wrestling matches with long guns. It never hurts to have some extra space for piling stuff on, too. After all, a workbench just isn't a workbench without at least a few piles of clutter.

Don't lose sleep over the bench surface. Gun cleaning is messy business and that nice, shiny, white Formica top will very soon become a hideous looking affair no matter how careful you are. Early on, my bench top was nicely varnished, the maple wood underneath glowing like fine cabinetry. That was short lived. The varnish has long since departed and now you can hardly tell that it's even wood. It's just a mottled grayish-brown with a deeply saturated patina from every bore cleaner, degreaser, and lubricant known to man. The point is, just a plain, unfinished wood top is fine. Fancy it up if you must, but if you're an avid shooter it won't stay pretty long. The one thing you don't want in a bench top is anything too hard. The harder it is, the more likely it will ding up a gunstock or break a dropped bottle. Same thing for protrusions such as edge molding; they only get in the way.

If space is a factor, with a little ingenuity you can devise some sort of fold-away or collapsible bench. Again, just be sure it's sturdy and stable. If you're fat with cash you can even buy one of the commercial takedown work benches that have all sorts of adjustments, clamping arrangements, and other bells and whistles.

A critical item for the bench top is some form of pad. Without a pad a gun slides around on the bench top like a curling stone on ice. A pad also prevents damage to both the gun and bench. For over forty years I've used a plain old cotton bath towel and see no reason to switch. A full-size towel folded in half lengthwise is just right for most rifles and shotguns and provides the perfect soft-but-not-squishy padding. When the towel gets embarrassingly nasty, run 'er through the washer. For smaller items such as handguns a computer mouse pad works pretty slick, too, though you have to be careful with certain aggressive chemicals that can turn the foam backing into goo.

You'll also need a plentiful and handy supply of rags. I have a simple paper towel rack mounted on the wall behind the bench which takes care of many mop up chores. I use the strongest, most pliable and absorbent paper towels I can find. Skimping here only causes frustration. Often, though, even the best paper towels just don't have the guts for the job. That's where a supply of cotton rags comes in. If you want to impress folks you can buy those fancy red shop rags at an automotive supply store. Otherwise just cut up the T-shirts the dog shredded while playing tug of war. Be sure the material is cotton, though. Synthetics don't absorb worth beans. Old flannel shirts work great, too.

LIGHTING

Good, strong lighting is one of the most critical elements of the work area. This is especially important for those of us more seasoned in years, when the old eagle eyes more resemble those of a bat. Much to-do has been made about the ill effects of fluorescent lighting. As I understand it, a fluorescent light continually flickers which, though unnoticeable to us, causes eye fatigue and headaches. Perhaps this would be an issue if we were cutting fine English scroll engraving on a Purdey shotgun but, hey, we're just cleaning gunk from guns. I like fluorescent lighting as it provides bright, even light over a large area. A note of caution: If hanging them overhead, be sure they're high enough that you don't whack them when flipping the gun end for end. I can testify that hunkering down under a shower of glass shards is more than a little disconcerting.

No matter what you use for general lighting, you'll also want some form of adjustable bench light for more detailed work. There are a jillion different styles available. Some are engineering marvels, a concoction of multiple arms, springs, and joints that can run several hundred dollars. At the other end of the scale

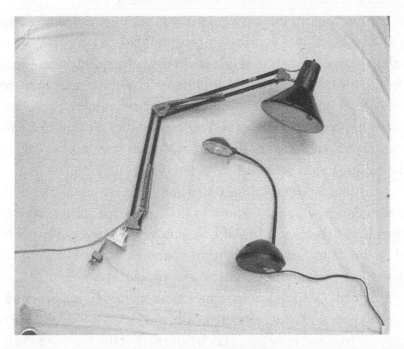

An adjustable bench light allows light to be directed exactly where needed. These can be as elaborate (and expensive) as a professional drafting light or as simple as a flex-tubing goose neck lamp costing under $10.

is the simple, flex tubing gooseneck type costing under twenty bucks. Take your pick.

TOOL ORGANIZATION

Few things are more annoying than having every task start with a scavenger hunt. It's so nice, not to mention a big timesaver, to have a place for everything and everything in its place. The key thing to keep in mind when designing tool storage is convenience. If it's not quick and easy to return an item to its designated place, you'll likely just shove it aside to be put away on that proverbial "someday." The someday pile is like a pair of rabbits, multiplying at an exponential rate, and soon you're back into the perpetual scavenger-hunt mode. Wall hangers, shelves, cabinets, and boxes can all serve to keep the clutter to a minimum as well as protect valuable tools.

I find one of the handiest ways to store gun cleaning tools and supplies is in a compartmented tool box. A mechanic's tool cabinet large enough to hold all of our tools and supplies would be just peachy but they're frightfully expensive and probably overkill for our needs. Hardware stores carry portable plastic tool boxes in a variety of styles and sizes. If you don't find just what you need there, head to the sporting goods store and check out the fishing tackle boxes.

To find a box of the right size and style, lay out all the items you intend to store in it—bore brushes, jags, special screwdrivers and allen wrenches, boxes of bore patches, whatever. Make a list of all the items. Also note their measurements. From this you can determine the number and sizes of compartments and drawers you'll need. Of special importance is a separate compartment for each caliber and gauge of bore brush and jag so you don't have to play the trial and error game each time to find the right one. Strive to have individual compartments for as many of the items as practical. What you don't want is simply a bottomless pit to throw stuff

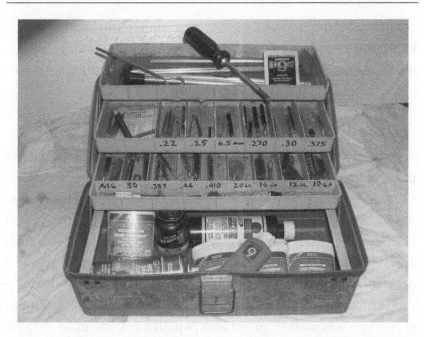

Compartmented tool or fishing-tackle boxes are inexpensive and perfect for storing cleaning and shooting supplies.

in. Boxes with adjustable compartments provide the most diversity. I don't store liquids such as bore cleaners and lubricants in the box, though, as they're bulky and, if tipped over, may leak. It's better to store these upright in a cabinet or on wall shelves.

I prefer to keep my common tools such as one piece bore rods, screwdrivers, files, hammers, chisels, saws, clamps, etc. hung up on the wall. There are all manner of hooks, spring clamps, gadgets, and gizmos available to hang just about anything that can be hung. I have an aversion to the pegboard system, though, as the hangers are always falling off. I prefer the hangers to be attached solidly to the wall. If you can do it without getting into too much trouble with the Missus, draw an outline on the wall of each tool. That way you can tell when Junior absconded with something and didn't bring it back.

If wall hanging isn't an option a multi-drawer cabinet may be the answer. Drawers can be designated for each tool grouping, one for screwdrivers, one for files, another for chisels and knives and so on.

RANGE BOX

As long as we're in the business of storage, now is a good time to put together a range box, too. A range box is just what the name implies, a portable box to hold all the tools and supplies you commonly take to the range. These may include cleaning items like a takedown bore rod, brushes, jags, solvents and patches, tools such as screw drivers, allen wrenches and pliers, and shooting gear like ear muffs, glasses, sandbags, targets, staple gun, tape, and felt-tip marker. Again, this is to eliminate the two-hour scavenger hunt every time you want to go out and pop off a few rounds. I strongly suggest dedicating these items to the range box even though they may be duplicated in the cleaning box or elsewhere. That way you just pick up the box, gun, and ammo and you're gone. No switching around, no forgetting stuff.

Select a range box just as you did the tool box. Lay everything out, make a list of the items, and note their measurements. Most likely you'll find the range box must be larger and sturdier than the cleaning box as things like ear muffs and sand bags take up a lot of room and the weight can add up fast. For weight and bulk reasons I don't transport ammo in the range box. It goes in another container.

An option to one humongous range box is several smaller ones, which help avoid hernias. They can be divided up in a number of ways depending on the type of shooting you do. One can hold big items like muffs, spotting scope, sandbags, stapler, and so on, with the other for tools and cleaning supplies. Still another can be geared toward black powder, if you're of that bent, with powder, caps, measure, bullets, etc.

While you can surely find something at the hardware, automotive, or sporting-goods store that will suffice, if you're the handy type you may wish to make your own custom range box. Using hardwood plywood of oak, cherry, or walnut will make you the envy of the range. Quarter-inch plywood is plenty thick. Figure out your overall dimensions, make the box all in one piece, and saw it apart on a table saw to form top and bottom. Then you can add dividers, made of one-eighth- or even one-sixteenth-inch plywood, as you please. Make her plenty beefy and use glue and screws rather than nails. Metal outside-corner braces really cinch things up. Use a piano hinge and suitcase handle and latches, all available at hardware stores. Beef up the handle and latch attachment with corresponding metal or wood plates on the inside of the box and use machine screws and nuts instead of wood screws.

Chapter 2

THERE'S NO TOOL LIKE THE RIGHT TOOL: TOOL SELECTION AND USE

VISES

Few things come more into play in gun tinkering than the vise. It's like having two extra hands, and super bionic ones at that. With a good vise there's no wrestling around with a gun, trying to pin it down in a half nelson so you can run a bore rod down its gullet. It holds parts securely, leaving our hands free to perform delicate operations. It grips things in a death hold while we reef, whack, and pound on them. A vise is a gun man's best friend.

You have several options in selecting a vise. The hands down best and most versatile is the standard bench vise. The essential thing here is to not go wimpy. I'm talking a big, monstrous, humongous, ore-boat anchor with a gaping jaw spread. This size allows us to grip most any gun part from any direction our heart desires. The mega vise has the guts so if a part REALLY needs

Some sort of fixture for holding guns and parts is essential. A large bench vise is the best but a portable gun clamp or an inexpensive gun cradle may fill your needs.

cinching down you can climb on it for all you're worth. Try that with a smaller vise and something's going to break. The new price of such a vise will make you weak in the knees but used ones still frequently show up at farm or machine shop auctions, often for next to nothing.

Invariably these vises have removable steel jaw covers. The steel wreaks havoc on guns, so take them off. Using them for a model, make identical ones out of hardwood. Hard maple is the best but oak, walnut, or something similar will suffice. Don't bother with softwoods like pine or fir; they will deform in nothing flat. Then cut pieces of thick leather to cover the wood jaw faces and glue them on with a contact adhesive. By using a contact adhesive, when the leather gives out you can just peel it off and install new ones.

If you have no intentions of getting that serious about things and only want something to hold a firearm for cleaning and maybe some bore sighting you have other options. There are portable "gun clamps" designed to hold either long guns or handguns that some folks even use as a makeshift machine rest for shooting. The simplest and most economical yet very effective holding fixture is a simple gun cradle. This is basically just a flat base with "V" blocks at each end in which the buttstock and forend rest. They start at around twenty bucks.

SCREWDRIVERS

There are screwdrivers and then there are screwdrivers. Quality screwdrivers are some of the most important tools you can own. On the other hand, poor screwdrivers are a gunsmith's nemesis. You can use the $1.99 hardware store versions to fix the door hinge or open paint cans but never, ever let them near your guns. Dinged up screw slots are an unforgivable sin and anyone that buggers up the screws on a fine firearm spends his afterlife in a very hot place. There's a lot of 'em down there, too, I might add.

The problem with standard screwdrivers is the sides of the blade taper at an angle to the tip. That's a manufacturing convenience and why the screwdriver only costs $1.99. Are the sides of a screw slot tapered? Of course not, they're straight as a church wall. Obviously, the tapered blade of the standard screwdriver only contacts the very upper edges of the screw slot. When a screw is being cantankerous, as so many are wont to, the edge of the slot gives way when you put the muscle to it. I already told you where you're going then.

The cure for this problem is to use hollow ground screwdrivers. Hollow ground means the screwdriver blade is shaped with a round grinding wheel which leaves the tip straight. This allows the tip to fully enter the slot and provides complete contact with

The tapered blade of a standard screwdriver (left) is notorious for damaging screws. Hollow-ground blades (right) are essential to prevent screw-slot damage.

the slot walls. It's a more expensive manufacturing procedure but it's beyond worth it. It's mandatory for gun work.

The other cause of screw slot damage is using the wrong size screwdriver blade. The blade must be the full width of the screw head and fit snugly into the slot with no slop. If the blade is too narrow or too thin you're begging for trouble. Unfortunately, there are no standards with screw slots. Some are so narrow the screwdriver blade must be paper thin. Others are so wide you could use a shovel instead of a screwdriver. With the seemingly infinite variety of screw-head sizes and slot widths found on gun screws it takes a considerable selection of screwdrivers to accommodate them.

Brownell's, the well known gunsmith supply firm in Montezuma, Iowa, is one of the better sources for high quality, hollow-ground screwdrivers for the firearm trade. They offer two basic screwdriver options: a full set of screwdrivers or a single handle with a set of interchangeable blades. Serious gunsmiths typically have a set of both. There's no substitute for a stout, one-piece screwdriver when dealing with an unusually tight or rusted-in screw. The interchangeable-blade model, however, is much more economical so you don't gulp as hard when you have to re-shape a blade to fit a particular screw. I find myself routinely grinding on these blades to obtain the perfect fit. The blades are also offered individually so you simply order more to replace the ones you ground into oblivion.

RESHAPING SCREWDRIVER BLADES

In theory, reshaping a hollow-ground screwdriver blade is a pretty simple task. It's done with a small, medium grit grinding wheel of one-inch to one-and-a-quarter inch in diameter. Such wheels,

Screwdrivers must fit the screw slot perfectly to avoid damage. Grind to size while retaining the hollow-ground shape with a small grinding wheel in an electric drill (the poor-man's lathe). The drill can be held in a vise or clamped to a bench top with "C" clamps.

designed to fit in an electric drill, are available at most hardware stores. Ideally, the wheel would be mounted in a lathe but few hobbyists are blessed with this luxury. That means we turn to the poor-man's lathe, an electric drill clamped in a large vise or secured to the bench with big "C" clamps.

Select a screwdriver blade just slightly thicker than the slot and carefully grind equal amounts from each side until it perfectly fits the slot. Wear your concentration cap for this because it's easier said than done. The sides must be kept uniform and straight because we can't have it thinner on one side than the other. If the blade is wider than the screw head it can be narrowed down at this time as well. Quality screwdrivers are made of tempered carbon steel so we also have to avoid heat build-up, or risk ruining the temper. That means only lightly grinding for a second or two, then dunking the blade in water. You can see excessive heat build-up by watching the color of the tip of the blade. If it turns tan you've borderline screwed up. If it turns blue you've just ruined it. The colors appear and change almost instantaneously so be on your toes. Also be sure to wear glasses as the high-carbon steel will throw a shower of sparks like Fourth of July fireworks.

Now, I suspect with you frugal types the light bulb has just come on. Why not just get cheap tapered screwdrivers and hollow grind them? If you're short on projects to occupy your time, this can be done using the same process. In many cases, however, inexpensive screwdrivers are made of inferior metal and can be either too soft or too hard. This may not be a factor with fairly large, thick blades. Get into tiny, thin blades, though, and the tip, if too soft, bends out of shape like cardboard. If too hard it's brittle and just snaps off, possibly damaging the gun in the process. You can get some idea of the hardness of a blade while grinding. The more sparks coming off, the harder it is. You want that "just right" in between. When all is said and done, though, unless money is a major factor just buy the real deal in the first place and be done with it.

ALLEN WRENCHES

In recent times we're seeing more socket-head screws on firearms. Once reserved solely for scope mounting systems, they're now appearing on action screws, trigger adjustments, and various other screws. We old curmudgeons who were born with real screwdrivers in our hands are having a hard time adjusting to that, but socket-head screws do have certain advantages. Because of the tight fit of wrench to socket the chance of screw-head damage is greatly reduced. The "L" shape of the wrench arguably provides better feel of the torque being applied as well as allowing more torque with less muscle. With allen wrenches it's also less likely that threads will be stripped or small screws broken because the wrench is sized in relation to the screw and will typically begin to bend before the screw gives way.

Allen wrench sets can be purchased in several configurations. One of the more common is a rig where they fold into a handle on the order of a many-bladed jackknife. You may also find them bound together on a split ring and, of course, they can be purchased just standing on their own as individual wrenches or sets. While the combo rigs may at first seem handy, they tend to be cumbersome and unwieldy to use. I much prefer a set of individual wrenches contained in a compartmented bag. After considerable use allen wrenches tend to lose their sharp edges where they engage the socket. This is particularly so with the small ones used in scope mounting. When a wrench shows sign of rounded edges or bending, discard it and get another.

HAMMERS

Another general tool indispensable to the gun tinker is hammers. I'm not talking your typical claw hammer, though. In gun work we use hammers to drive pins in and out and for judicious coaxing on a multitude of stubborn parts. For pins, a small to mid-size machinist's hammer in conjunction with a punch is the norm. In some cases these hammers are also used to drive prying instruments gently to free stuck parts.

On occasion we may need to give a particular part a direct whack with the hammer to get its attention. Though I say whack, it's usually more a series of light taps. Obviously, a metal hammer for this task will ding up the bluing and very likely damage the part. There are hammers available with heads made of more

A variety of hammers are needed in gun work. The author finds the most useful to be (left to right): small ball peen, nylon head, wood mallet, machinist's hammer, copper head.

benign materials like copper, brass, wood, leather, lead, and plastic. The best by far for gun work is a head of plastic such as nylon or similar material. Copper, brass, and lead leaves a metallic mark on the bluing. Wood, leather, and lead are too soft for many applications. A plastic head does not deform, leaves no mark on bluing, and won't damage normal firearm metals. What more could one ask? Again, a gunsmith supply firm such as Brownell's is a good source.

BRUSHES/STEEL WOOL/SCRAPERS/ETC.

Guns have a remarkable affinity for getting all gunked up in the innards. Most of the source of this crud is powder residue and dried out lubricants. Not only can this stuff be tenacious, it tends to hole up in the most inaccessible of places. Typically, the best way to defeat it is with solvents and various types of brushes. We have to be a bit careful here, though, lest we harm the bluing or, in the case of stainless steel, the surface polish.

The first step in brush selection is to understand the potential brushes have for gun damage. Bluing is pretty tough stuff but steel brush bristles over .003-inches diameter can scratch it, especially if manipulated with zeal. Steel bristles much over .005-inches diameter will dig into bluing like a chicken scratchin' in the dirt. A fine brass or bronze bristle brush won't damage the bluing, per se, but will leave a copper or yellow wash on the metal surface that is difficult to remove. This is especially noticeable on bluing. Steel wool is also commonly used for gunk removal. As far as bluing goes, you're safe to moderately scrub with No. 0000 steel wool and you can usually get away with some brief, light scrubbing with No. 000. More coarse than that and the bluing is in definite jeopardy. Nylon bristles as found on toothbrushes and plastic bore brushes are totally benign, they would hardly ruffle a chickadee's feathers.

Surprisingly, it's difficult to find good brushes small enough for gun work, which means toothbrush size or even smaller. Brownell's carries a few that fit our damage avoidance criteria but they could stand to be smaller and offered in a wider variety of shapes and contours. One of the best places to find such specialty brushes is in the custom machining industry. However, since we're just cleaning a few guns here, most of us can make do with the more readily available brushes.

A couple of small, stainless-steel wire brushes will never languish unused for long. Toothbrushes are also a staple of gun cleaning. The nylon bristles are impervious to all solvents commonly used with firearms. Check out the drug store racks and get a selection of sizes and contours. While we're here, a note on

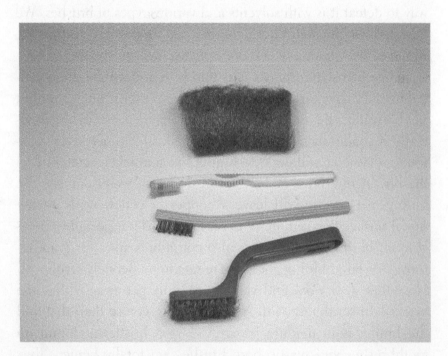

Brushes in a variety of sizes, shapes, and materials are some of the gun tinker's most-used tools. Steel wool also has limited use.

brushes: I dedicate some for the really down and dirty work. Others I save for the more uptown jobs like brushing dust and debris from exterior cracks and crevices, checkering and the like where you'd just as soon not leave a coating of black goo. As for steel wool, you won't find it as useful as one might think. When fine enough to avoid damage (the No. 0000 and No. 000 previously discussed) it doesn't have a lot of "go get 'em." For gunk removal purposes it's not much better than a rag. It also leaves a trail of little wire strands wherever it goes that can cause functioning problems. Have some, for sure, because it's unsurpassed for removing microscopic rust from metal surfaces, but you needn't get carried away with your supply. Pipe cleaners and, most of all, cotton-tipped swabs are handy for hard-to-reach places.

Finally we come to our most serious crud-fighting weapon, scrapers. There are times when we can soak and scrub till we're blue in the face yet some stuff just won't give up. No worries, we'll just dig it out. This is largely reserved for internal use because any metal scraper will gouge bluing in a heartbeat. For general grubbing purposes the small hobby knives with replaceable blades, commonly called X-Acto knives, are hard to beat. The pointed blade gets into nooks, crannies, and corners while the flat and rounded blades work better on larger areas. For really hard to reach places, suck up to your dentist and have him save his old dental picks and scrapers for you. These come in a variety of twisted shapes and contours that can reach anywhere a gun has to offer. Of course, small screwdrivers and such have their place as well.

One trick I've found for scraping delicate surfaces such as bluing and stock finish is wood scrapers. Popsicle sticks and tongue depressors, whatever wood they're made of—probably birch—are my favorites. Grind the rounded end flat across but don't put a beveled edge on it. When the scraping edge gets dull just grind it back a bit. These won't harm bluing a bit, but tread lightly on stocks.

BORE RODS

There are two schools of thought regarding bore-cleaning rods, both concerning potential bore damage from the rod. One school believes a rod made of a soft material, whether it be aluminum, brass, or plastic coated steel, will become embedded with all manner of things from bullet-jacket material and powder residue to sand, volcanic dust, and meteor fragments. Then what you have is an abrasive rod eating away at the rifling with each pass. The other school feels that's all a bunch of hog puckey. They believe steel rods, being harder than the barrel steel, will wear the rifling, and that soft rods are the lesser of two evils. Well, I suppose there's a third school, too, those who don't give a rip one way or the other and just use whatever is on sale at Wal-Mart.

In a sense both the soft-rod and hard-rod advocates are right. Grit can become embedded in aluminum, brass and plastic-coated rods and damage the bore with each pass. In addition, aluminum begins oxidizing very quickly if not protected from the air. What is aluminum oxide? It's the most common grinding, sanding, and polishing abrasive in use today. If an aluminum rod is not cleaned and oiled before each use it could cause undue rifling wear. On the other hand a rod made of material harder than the barrel steel, such as a hardened steel rod, will eventually wear the rifling as well. The key to cleaning the bore properly is to prevent the rod from coming in contact with the bore to begin with. Then it doesn't matter what material the rod is made of. This is the job of the bore guide, which we'll discuss a bit further on.

For shop use, a one-piece rod is generally best. Their rigidity makes them user friendly and you don't have to mess around finding and matching various sections. Takedown rods, though they can certainly be used for general cleaning, are more suited to the range box and hunting trips. The most critical aspect of a bore rod used for rifles is a quality, ball-bearing mounted handle. The handle must spin freely while under pressure to allow the rod to turn with the rifling. Otherwise, the rifling will either continually unscrew the brush or jam it so tight you can't get it off, depending on the direction of the rifling twist. This isn't important with shotguns and short handgun barrels, though.

Another thing to watch for when selecting bore rods is the threads for attaching brushes and other accoutrements. Here in the U.S. the standard threads are 8-32 for rifles and handguns, 5-40 for .17 caliber and 5-16-inch-27 for shotguns. I use the term "standard" somewhat loosely because a few manufacturers, for whatever reason, choose to make life difficult for us. Some small bore rods have 8-36 threads. You may also encounter 7-32, 10-32, or even 12-28 threads on rifle rods. Then there are the foreign-made rods with metric threads. I strongly advise you to stick with the standard thread configurations because that's what you're most likely to find at Bubba's Gun & Sandwich Shop down on the corner. Also, many of the specialty brushes and other accoutrements are only available with standard threads.

For decades when I went on fly-in or pack-in hunting trips I made a cleaning arrangement from a string with a weight on one end and a proper sized patch on the other. Of course, it wasn't a serious cleaning outfit but sufficed to get rain water and spiders out of the bore and give it a light coat of rust preventive. A few years ago somebody much smarter than me took that concept further. The string was enlarged to a soft, tapered rope. At the upper end the rope is bore sized and serves as a long bore swab. Woven into the middle of this swab is a bristle brush. Voila! Brush and patch all in one. When it gets dirty simply wash it with dish soap. The most commonly available one of this style is called the

"Hoppe's Bore Snake" and is carried by most gun shops. Not only are they handy while on the trail, you just may find them the bore cleaning implement of choice because they eliminate all worries of cleaning rod damage and wear. Of course, a separate one is required for differing calibers and gauges.

BORE GUIDES

Few casual shooters use bore guides, but they should. Regardless whether going from the muzzle or breech, it's nigh on to impossible to hand feed a rod perfectly straight into the barrel so that it doesn't rub on the bore at the entry point. I'll venture a guess that more barrels are worn out in this manner than shot out. A bore guide is simply a fixture in which the rod runs through that centers the rod in the bore. With the rod supported on one end by the brush or jag and on the other end by the bore guide it can't come in contact with the bore. Any chance of wear or damage from the rod is alleviated.

For guns that must be cleaned from the muzzle end the bore guide is on the order of a tapered plug with a hole in the middle

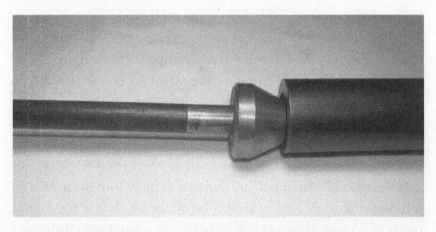

Bore damage from cleaning rods is a very real problem. When cleaning from the muzzle a simple, cone-shaped bore guide prevents the rod from contacting the bore.

that fits in the muzzle and guides the rod. You may need several to accommodate various bore diameters. The preferred way, when possible, is to clean a barrel from the breech end. This same style of guide works for any barrel that is directly accessible from the breech such as pumps and semi-autos with removable barrels, break actions, and muzzle loaders with the breech plug removed.

Bolt actions are also commonly cleaned from the breech. Here things aren't quite so simple because of all that action sticking out behind the barrel and getting in the way. The most common bore guide for bolt actions is a tube affair that replaces the bolt. The rod runs through the guide which aligns it with the bore and prevents it from bearing on the critical throat area directly in front of the chamber. Most brands will fit a number of different rifle models but unless it's of the adjustable type you need separate ones for short and long actions. Inexpensive plastic models such as

Bolt-action bore guides replace the bolt and center the rod in the bore to prevent rifling damage. This plastic bore guide from MTM is widely available and costs less than $10. Professional-grade models, some adjustable to fit a variety of actions, are available though gunsmith-supply firms.

the MTM Bore Guide cost less than ten bucks. More high-falutin' brands can run three times that much or more.

BORE BRUSHES

We are faced with somewhat of a dilemma when it comes to bore cleaning. The stuff that accumulates in a bore—powder, copper, lead, and perhaps plastic residue—can be some very tenacious stuff. It would be nice if we could use a really stiff, hard, go-get-'em brush that would aggressively dig into the accumulated crud. The problem is such a brush would scratch the barrel steel, causing permanent damage. It would also roughen the surface, promoting even more fouling. Therefore we must compromise with something softer.

For over a century the good ol' bronze brush has been the standard for bore cleaning. As its timelessness attests, in conjunction with solvent it does a pretty good job of scrubbing crud from the bore. Of course, when purchasing one be sure to get the proper size for the caliber of your gun. Resist the temptation to get the next size bigger in hopes of a little more oomph. You just end up with kinked, less effective bristles. I've not noticed a big quality difference between the commonly available brands so I just go with whatever the local shop carries. Before purchasing remember to check the thread size as we discussed in the bore rod section. If you have a rod with odd ball threads you may have to order brushes from the manufacturer or a gunsmith-supply firm.

There is one problem with the bronze brush, however. The more aggressive bore solvents formulated to dissolve copper residue eat them up faster than a kid can down a Snickers bar. With these solvents it's better to use a nylon brush. The nylon bristles aren't as stiff and "scratchy" as bronze brushes so it takes more scrubbing, but the bristles are impervious to the solvents.

Some of the strongest proponents of nylon brushes are the serious target shooters who feel the nylon bristles are friendlier to the rifling. Most casual shooters need not worry about rifling wear with bronze brushes, if such a thing is even possible, but I guess if you're cleaning the bore every day, going exclusively with nylon wouldn't hurt.

One type of brush that has been embroiled in controversy ever since its inception is the steel bore brush. Made of stainless steel, they are impervious to all solvents and do provide significantly more scrubbing power over standard bronze and nylon brushes. However, many fear they will scratch the bore and, with extended use, cause rifling damage. I have these fears myself and have only used steel brushes on revolver chambers and chromed shotgun bores so I can't voice a valid opinion. A quicky survey of a handful of professionals did little to clear the water. It was a general consensus that the steel brushes were slightly softer than most barrel steels so they probably wouldn't scratch the bore. My observation with using them in revolver chambers supports this. Some experts had no worries with using them. Others, though, expressed concern that extended use might cause rifling wear over time. Even some of the suppliers caution against overuse. Sorry, you'll have to decide for yourself on this one.

There is a version of steel brush that is less likely to cause bore problems. Named the Tornado Brush, its construction resembles a coil spring wound around a central shaft. Only the smooth sides of the "spring" contact the bore so, at least in theory, it shouldn't be as inclined to scratch as a standard shaped brush. This is just the ticket for grubbing out plastic wad residue from shotgun bores. It's also available in rifle and handgun sizes but I don't see how the wire coil could reach into the rifling grooves, especially down in the corners which are the biggest problem areas, so what's the point?

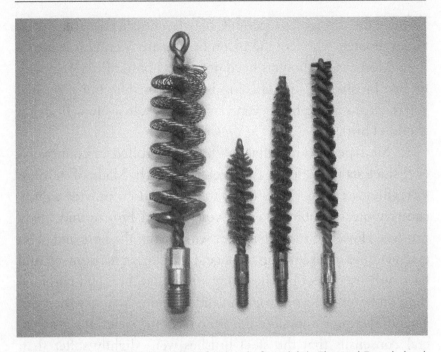

Bore brushes are available in a variety of styles. (Left to right): The steel Tornado brush is popular with shotgunners for removing plastic-wad fouling. Stainless-steel brushes provide more scrubbing action than bronze brushes but some people fear bore damage from extended use. The standard bronze brush is inexpensive and suitable with mild solvents. Nylon brushes are a must with copper bore solvent, which destroys bronze brushes.

While on the subject of brushes, we might as well discuss chamber brushes. These are sized to match the various cartridges rather than the bore diameter. Unlike bores, which accumulate bullet jacket and lead residue, chamber fouling is just light powder residue from escaping gasses, but they still need cleaning and protection from rust. With straight walled cartridges or those nearly so, regular bore cleaning cares for the chamber well enough. If the cartridge is bottle necked, though, it takes some special effort. With bolt guns and others accessible from the rear this can be done with the regular bore brush by removing the bore guide and applying sideways pressure. Guns that must be cleaned from the muzzle, however, will require the use of a chamber brush. These you will likely have to order from the manufacturer or a gunsmith-supply firm. They are severely compressed while going through the bore and don't last long, so order several.

Last but not least is a specialty item for handguns, the Lewis Lead Remover. Once upon a time in my checkered past I was a law-enforcement shooting instructor, teaching conservation officers, sheriff deputies, and state troopers combat shooting as well as training other firearm instructors. Of course, I had to shoot at least equal to my most proficient students so I had a virtually limitless supply of handgun ammo at my disposal to keep in tune. Man, did I shoot! My old Smith revolver digested uncountable thousands of rounds. The problem was all the freebie ammo was

The brass screen of the Lewis Lead Remover very effectively removes lead build-up from revolver chambers and barrel forcing cones.

lead-bulleted target rounds and after a day of shooting there was enough lead built up in the chambers and bore to start my own foundry. This was before the days of high-powered, advanced bore cleaners and that lead stuck like it was soldered on. That's when I discovered the Lewis Lead Remover.

The Lewis Lead Remover is essentially a tight fitting rubber jag utilizing a bronze screen rather than a cloth patch. The screen scrapes the lead away without damaging the gun. I found it most effective for chamber cleaning where lead is especially prone to build up in the forcing-cone area. In the bore the screen could not effectively reach into the sharp corners of the rifling. It was a good thing to start with but eventually a brush was in order. There is also an attachment to clean the forcing cone at the rear of the barrel. While today's bore solvents have improved at lead removal, the Lewis Lead Remover is still one of the best ways to deal with lead build-up in cylinders and forcing cones.

JAGS

Jags are the unsung heroes of gun cleaning. Surprisingly, few people realize how effective a good jag is for bore cleaning. I suspect this stems from the slotted patch loops erroneously called jags that often come with the inexpensive aluminum cleaning kits and that are so popular.

The typical jag is a button shaped affair that screws into the bore rod for holding cloth patches. The jag is just slightly under bore diameter so when the patch is draped over the end it pushes the cloth tightly against the bore and into the rifling grooves. This jag/patch assembly is used to apply solvent to the bore, scrub away fouling, wipe away the gunk left from brushing, dry the bore, and to apply a thin, uniform coat of oil or rust preventive.

Jags come in a variety of materials, the most common being brass, aluminum, nylon, or polycarbonate. I feel brass is the best,

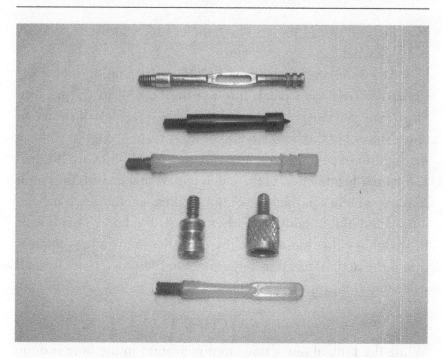

Jags are used in conjunction with cloth patches to apply and remove solvent and rust preventives from the bore as well as provide cleaning action. They are available in a variety of styles and materials. The author prefers those made of metal rather than plastic.

followed by aluminum. With a tight fitting patch, as it should be, a jag is subjected to a certain amount of stress. In my experience the nylon and other plastic jags are prone to breaking, perhaps not early on but sooner or later. They may be a buck cheaper but what's a buck when you consider a good metal jag will last the better part of a lifetime?

There's always a number of ways to skin a cat and there are other style jags. Some have a slotted tip in front of the button jag. This holds the patch in place even when it's not in the bore. Just be sure the distance between the slot and jag is not so far the patch doesn't fully cover the jag. There are also long jags designed for the patch to be wrapped around rather than draped over the end. I find these to be tedious and a bit trickier to use, but pick whatever suits your fancy.

As for the aforementioned slotted patch loop, it, too, is designed for running a patch through the bore. It just doesn't do any of the previously listed tasks as well as a jag. It will suffice to apply solvent to the bore, dry the bore, and apply oil; but without the tight fit of patch to bore the cleaning capabilities are limited. I suppose the attraction of the patch loop is that it holds the patch in place whether in the bore or not. With a jag, the patch has the annoying habit of falling off when it exits the bore. That means the patch is either lost to a grubby, gritty floor or you have to dig it out of the action. As far as I'm concerned, though, that's a small price to pay for superior function.

PATCHES

While the bulk of our serious rootin' around in the bore is done with the brush, we still need something to remove the crud the brush loosened up. This is one of the primary job descriptions of the patch. It may seem silly to devote space to such a lowly item but there's more to a patch than one may think. To rank quality status a patch must be highly absorbent in order to carry a good quantity of solvent to the bore as well as suck up all the juicy crud left from brushing. It must also be thick and pliable enough to reach down into the corners of the rifling yet not so thick that it's too tight in the bore with a standard jag. It should also provide some scrubbing action of its own. Of course, it's nice if it doesn't leave a trail of lint everywhere it goes, too. That's asking a lot.

One of the most tried-and-true patch materials is cotton flannel. That's what you'll most likely find on the local shelves. They're relatively inexpensive, highly absorbent, and the fluffy texture reaches into rifling recesses better than any other comparable material. On the flip side, flannel patches don't provide as much scrubbing action as some other materials and if of poor quality they tend to shed lint.

Forever price conscious, nowadays some patch manufacturers are resorting to synthetic materials. These may look like cotton flannel but they are not as absorbent as cotton and are second-rate at best.

Another patch material that has its place is cotton twill. Twill refers to the way the fibers are woven together, which is a tight but rather coarse weave. These do not have the fluffy appearance of flannel. They are smoother with distinct weave ridges. Still quite soft, they reach into rifling grooves fairly well and the ridges provide a more aggressive scrubbing action than flannel. They don't absorb and carry quite as much solvent as flannel but if you're looking for more cleaning power twill is worth considering. The ideal is a selection of both.

A critical aspect of patches is using the correct size. Too large and they bind in the bore, making it difficult or impossible to push the rod through. An excessively tight fit also squeezes all of the solvent out of the patch, leaving the juice running down into the action while you scrub away fruitlessly with a dry patch. If undersized, the fit is too loose, providing little cleaning action and the patch may even come off in the bore. With a proper fitting patch you should feel moderate resistance while pushing the rod through the bore but you shouldn't have to bear down on it. Keep a selection of patch sizes on hand to fit all the calibers and gauges you anticipate cleaning.

MAKING PATCHES

One thing immediately noticeable is how you go through patches faster than popcorn on Super Bowl Sunday. A typical hundred-pack at three or four bucks may seem inconsequential but you can use a dozen or more on just one gun. Ten cleaning sessions and they're gone. To put it in even sharper perspective, say you have three rifles of differing calibers, a couple of handguns—.38 and .44 calibers—a 20 gauge upland shotgun, and a 12 gauge trap gun. That's a fairly modest gun collection. Buying bulk packs of 1,000 patches each to cover these guns would cost in the neighborhood of $150. That's a lot of beer and peanuts.

Being a miserly curmudgeon, I make my own. Of course, the material must be similar to the commercial patches, that is, white so we can see the amount of fouling, cotton for absorbency, and close to the same thickness. Obviously, to realize financial gains we can't go out and buy cloth. For a source of free cloth it helps to have a dog like my Brittany. A lively game of tug of war with your old T-shirt ensures enough holes and tears that you can finally retire it with good conscience. Voila again! A happy dog and patch material all in one.

Commercial patches are sometimes cut round rather than square. Round patches do provide a perfect fit on the jag but you

PATCH SIZE CHART

CAL./GA.	SIZE
.17 -.223	7/8"
.243 – .270	1 3/8"
7mm - .357	1 3/4"
.360 – 20 ga.	2 1/2"
16 – 10 ga.	3"

size may need to be adjusted depending on patch thickness

could make a career out of meticulously cutting out circles with scissors, not to mention wasting a lot of cloth. Square patches seem to work just as well. Simply cut the cloth in strips of the appropriate width then lop the strips into squares. You can even do it while watching TV. The accompanying chart lists the standard patch sizes for the various calibers. This may vary slightly according to the material thickness you're using. Try a couple test patches before you spend all evening whacking up cloth into the wrong size. It's also possible your chosen cloth may be too thick or thin to work at all. Test first.

ELECTROCHEMICAL BORE CLEANING SYSTEMS

Since this doesn't fit into any of the previous categories let's stick these modern marvels in here. Once thought of as a tool for professional gunsmiths, electrochemical cleaning systems like Outers

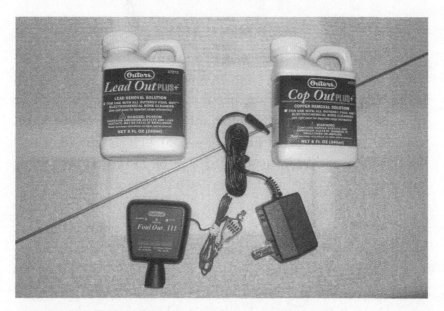

Electrochemical bore cleaning units such as Outers Foul Out are now reasonably priced and are beyond compare for removing copper-jacket and lead fouling.

Foul Out are now priced within everyone's reach. Running just a tad over one hundred bucks, they are the ultimate for removing bullet jacket material and lead build up from bores. This may seem awfully pricey but for those wanting to wring every bit of accuracy out of their rifle or handgun this is the answer. No other method compares to electronic cleaning for removing fouling from the bore.

Utilizing a combination of electricity and chemicals, it works like metal electroplating only in reverse. Instead of plating an object with copper or lead, it de-plates it. A special rod is inserted into the bore along with the appropriate chemical and the bore sealed with "O" rings. Simply plug it in and go catch the evening news. Within an hour, give or take, electrical current magically transports the metal fouling from the bore to the rod. Swab the bore out, give it a light hit of rust preventive, and that chore is history.

BORE LIGHTS

Other than the obvious gobs of loose powder fouling, bore fouling is pretty hard to see. Copper, lead, and plastic wad material scrub off onto the bore more like thin plating rather than chunks and often it's barely visible to the untrained eye. Barrel types that can be viewed straight through such as bolt action rifles and break-action or takedown shotguns can be inspected by holding one end up to a light and looking down the other end.

However, guns such as lever actions, revolvers and other types that don't allow this straight through view get trickier. One solution is to put something white like a cleaning patch or piece of paper in the action to reflect light into the bore. Much better is some sort of light source to shine from the inaccessible end while we look down the muzzle. For large caliber firearms like muzzleloaders and shotguns a small, AAA battery penlight can simply be

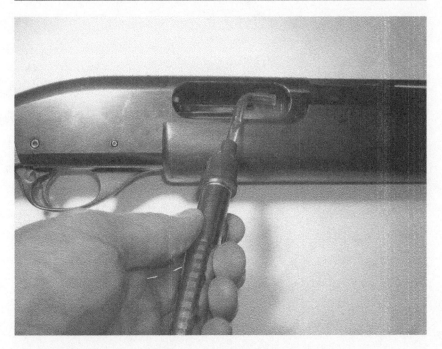

A bore light only costs a few bucks and is essential for detailed inspection of bores that don't allow a straight-through view.

slid down the bore from the muzzle end. For smaller bore diameters the answer is a specially designed bore light that bends its beam around a corner, if you will. The tip is inserted into the action with the bent beam directed up the bore while we view from the other end. These are typically available at well-stocked gun shops and gunsmith supply firms for just a few bucks.

Chapter 3

IT'S ALL IN THE JUICE: SOLVENTS, LUBRICANTS, AND RUST PREVENTIVES

BORE CLEANERS

Ah, the good old days. You know, back when kids walked a mile to school barefoot and the heady aroma of Hoppe's No. 9 went with guns like the smell of turkey with Thanksgiving. My how things have changed. Of course, Hoppe's No. 9 is still with us but now it's bobbing down the marketing stream amongst an immense flood of competitors. Powder solvents must be a lucrative business because it seems everyone is trying his hand at it, each one proclaiming superiority in one way or another.

While the vast array of bore cleaners seems overwhelming, it's really not that complicated. In simpler times a bore cleaner was a bore cleaner, period. Today, many are formulated for a specific task, like removing copper or lead. Hey, it's the age of specialization. I'll tell you straight out that I'm not about to try and cover every bore cleaner on the market. Brands not only come and go like yesterday's news, but I'd surely overlook some and ruffle someone's feathers. Instead, we'll just lump them into several categories.

First are the good old standard bore solvents like Hoppe's No. 9 or Outers Nitro Solvent. These are general purpose bore cleaners designed to remove powder fouling and minor build-up of copper jacket material, bullet lead, and perhaps plastic wad fouling. They are relatively mild and won't harm most stock finishes or bluing and they can be left to soak in the bore for days without risk of bore damage. Most are fairly inexpensive.

A solvent in this category is the best choice for routine gun cleaning. They do a good job as long as the gun is cleaned soon after shooting while fouling is still easily removed. No matter how often we use them there's little worry about gun damage or health hazards. Frankly, in my estimation all the established

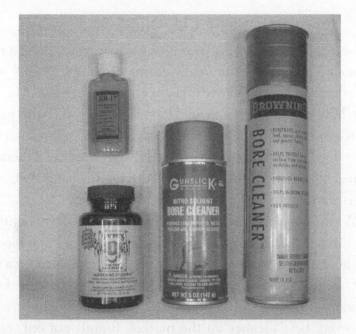

Standard bore solvents such as these remove most fouling if the gun is immediately cleaned after shooting and they are harmless to metal and most stock finishes.

name brands perform equally well. I can't say the same, however, for all the newcomers on the scene. Most perform satisfactorily but a few have proven disappointing. Those don't last long.

Next in line is what I call the aggressive bore cleaners. Shooter's Choice Bore Cleaner and Hoppe's Bench Rest-9 are a couple common examples in this category. These are the Arnold Schwarzeneggers of bore cleaners. They are still all-purpose solvents but have noticeably more muscle than standard bore cleaners. These are best used on excessively fouled bores or those that have gone long periods of time without cleaning where the fouling is set up really hard. "Ugh! Bigger better, why not use them all of the time?" Because nearly all of these will damage stock finish and, if allowed to stand in the bore too long, some may even attack the barrel steel. Also, most are quite fumey

Gunslick's Ultra Kleenz and Shooter's Choice are representative of solvents utilizing more aggressive chemicals for tough cleaning chores. They may cause metal damage if left in the bore too long and most will damage stock finish. J-B Bore Cleaner and Remington Brite Bore contain mild abrasives to remove tenacious fouling and polish the bore.

and nearly all pose some degree of health risk if proper safety precautions aren't followed. Adequate ventilation, protective aprons, and glasses and rubber gloves are the norm when using these solvents. Why subject the guns and ourselves to all this when we don't need something this aggressive? I save these for the really tough jobs and, of course, follow all precautions on the label to the letter.

Another type of bore cleaner that has a certain following contains a mild abrasive. J-B Bore Cleaning Compound has been around almost since fouling began and still leads the field in this category. Remington Bore Cleaner and Break-Free Bore Paste are other common brands utilizing abrasive. The abrasive is suspended in either a liquid or paste solvent and provides extra scrubbing action to help remove all types of fouling. Admittedly, it sounds a little scary to be scrubbing around inside a rifled barrel with an abrasive. J-B makes the claim that since its inception in the 1960's it "hasn't damaged an inch of rifling yet." Firearm legends like Warren Page and Jim Carmichel have also endorsed J-B in the past. That said, I know some equally knowledgeable and experienced shooters who won't even let an abrasive bore cleaner in the house.

I sit somewhere in the middle. For a really great-shooting barrel with little tendency to foul I don't use abrasive cleaners. However, with the average, run of the mill barrel I do use them on occasion and have noticed no ill effects. I don't use them for every cleaning, though. Something I've always wondered about but never got around to trying is if regular use of J-B, which is one of the most abrasive in this group, in conjunction with a tight fitting patch might actually serve as a lap to polish an exceptionally rough bore over time. If it did so without excessive rifling wear, fouling tendencies should lessen and accuracy improve. There's an experiment for someone with a bum barrel and lots of time.

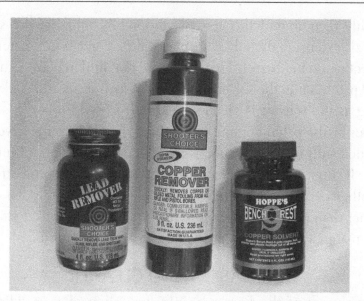

Powder residue is quite easy to remove but lead and bullet-jacket material can be extremely difficult. Solvents formulated specifically for these tasks are far superior to standard bore cleaner but are very aggressive. Follow all label precautions.

Last but not least are the specialty solvents that have come into vogue. These are pretty much what their labels state—lead remover, copper remover, plastic wad solvent, and so on. Obviously, you resort to these to solve a particular problem. An avid target shooter's rifle is free of powder fouling but the patch still keeps coming out green or blue, indicating bullet jacket metal is still present. He brings out the copper remover. A cop spends a day at the range shooting target wadcutters and there's enough lead built up in his revolver cylinder's forcing cones to make a boat anchor. It's time for the lead remover. A trap shooter's shotgun barrel looks like a melting pot at a plastics factory. Bring on the wad solvent. Just keep in mind, these are very aggressive solvents. Read the labels carefully and heed all precautions and safety warnings.

A final note on solvents. Most of the liquid bore solvents come in both bottle and aerosol form. For general shop use I highly recommend the aerosol version. By utilizing the straw nozzle extension the solvent can be squirted on a brush, patch, or directly into the barrel. That way we're not dunking dirty brushes and patches into the solvent and turning it all black and yucky. As long as the solvent is clean we can tell when the bore is truly clean by the patch coming out with no discoloring. I reserve the bottled stuff for when space is a problem, such as on a hunting trip. If you must use bottled solvent, pour a small amount off into another container for brush dunking and discard any left over rather than pouring it back into the bottle. And be sure to follow the manufacturer's instructions for safe and proper disposal.

DEGREASERS AND CLEANERS

Moving out of the bore and into the action offers a different cleaning challenge. Once into the guts of the action we find an incredible mass of gobbeldy-gook consisting of burned powder, dried lubricant, weed seeds, pine cones, a few spiders, and perhaps a shed snake skin. In the old days we used to just dunk the whole works into a can of gasoline and let 'er soak a day or two. A few folks fried their brains sniffing too many fumes and the occasional house went up in flames but that was just an accepted hazard of the job. Nowadays, the strict injunction would be, *"Don't try this at home!"* We have degreasers and action cleaners today that are much more user friendly.

Just about every manufacturer of gun cleaning products has a degreaser in its product line. Birchwood Casey Gun Scrubber, Hoppe's Cleaner/Degreaser, Tetra Action Blaster, Remington Rem Action Cleaner, and Shooter's Choice Quick Scrub III are just a few examples commonly found on gun-shop shelves. This stuff is God's gift to the gun world but many shooters fail to take advantage of it. The combination of solvent and pressure spray dissolves old lubricant and other crud and washes it away all in

Evaporating degreasers make short work of fouling and dried lubricant accumulated in the action and other areas without leaving a residue film.

one. It's also great for flushing powder solvent, water, or anything else out from behind moving parts in preparation for oiling. That often eliminates the need to disassemble parts. In most cases you'll still need to do some scrubbing with cotton-tipped swabs, rags, toothbrushes and whatnot but these products do work very well. After doing their job these solvents quickly evaporate, leaving no residue behind. As with bore cleaners, I find the name brands pretty much equal. You can select them by brand loyalty, most pleasing odor, least odor, or whatever is available at the moment.

A strong word of caution is in order with these aerosol degreasers. They're under considerable pressure and when sprayed into an action or on a part the solvent invariably ricochets all over the shop. This is especially so when utilizing the plastic straw nozzle extensions supplied with them. It seems as often as not a stream of solvent comes right back into your face. Always wear protective glasses, apron, long sleeve shirt, and rubber gloves. Whenever spraying into recesses such as actions, be sure to hold the part in such a way that any spray back is directed away from you. And as always, be certain your work area is adequately ventilated.

LUBRICANTS

Man, you thought bore solvents were confusing? You ain't seen nothin' yet. In a quick perusal of the Brownell's catalog I found over thirty lubricants designated for firearms! I doubt even someone with a lubricant master's degree could sort them all out, much less me. I've been working at it for over forty years, though, and have some general observations to pass on.

Like with bore solvents, I lump lubricants into categories. First are the simple liquid oils like Hoppe's Lubricating Oil. These are pretty much just plain old oil, though most have additives that prevent them from thickening or freezing in cold temperatures. They've served us well ever since we stopped killing sperm whales for their oil and still do a darn good job of keeping things moving and rust at bay. Once we get past these simple oils, though, things go absolutely nuts.

A lot of folks have laid awake at night trying to figure out what else could be put in oil to make it better. It seems the market is awash in a plethora of concoctions containing everything from Teflon and silicone to bat's wings and rattlesnake venom. Some are endorsed by Navy Seals, others by Army Rangers and who knows who all. The ones that come in liquid form in a bottle, I lump into one category. Of the ones I've tried, whether they're bolstered with Teflon, molybdenum disulfide, silicone, or some other witch's brew, all seem to have roughly the same attributes and drawbacks.

Lubricants come in a variety of formulations. Some are simple oils, many employ perfor-mance enhancing additives. Some are dry after they evaporate and others are heavy greases. All have their place.

A somewhat similar category to these is spray lubricants like the ever-popular WD-40, Outers Tri-Lube, Tri-Flow, Break-Free CLP, and on and on. With these it's hard to control the spray so they're best suited for large items like bolts. For small parts or putting it only in specific places, spray a cotton swab or rag and transfer it to the desired location. Many folks use these as rust preventives, too. While they work to a degree, specially formulated rust preventives are better.

The problem with nearly all liquid lubricants is they dry out over time and become gummy. It seems the fancier the concoctions the faster they dry out and the gummier they become. Some become gooey in a matter of weeks. Many of the aerosols seem particularly prone to this. Others may take several months. If a gun is frequently cleaned and re-lubed this isn't a problem. Let a heavily oiled gun sit idle over the winter, though, and it may even be nonfunctional come spring. Keep this in mind if you oil the bore after cleaning. Too much oil sitting too long could cause pressures to jump into the danger zone if it's not removed before shooting. In fact, any amount of oil in the bore should be removed before the gun is shot.

To get around some of the ills plaguing liquid lubricants, dry lubricants may be an option. The simplest of these is just plain powdered graphite, the stuff pencil lead is made from. More high-tech examples would be Dri-Slide, which utilizes molybdenum disulfide, and Bore Tech's Tef-Dri, which employs Teflon. Most of the dry lubricants come in a liquid or paste carrier that soon evaporates. Used sparingly, they do not gum up too badly or collect dust. They are also great in extreme cold weather, like on that musk-ox hunt to Ellesmere Island. Though quality liquid lubricants claim not to freeze, there is a limit and at the very least most will noticeably stiffen when the temp approaches the half-century below-zero mark. One thing dry lubricants don't do well is prevent rust.

While liquid or dry lubricants are best suited for most firearm applications, there are places where grease is superior. Grease stays where you put it, is much less prone to drying out, gumming up, or breaking down over time and is an excellent corrosion inhibitor. A quality grease hangs in there quietly doing its job for years. The downsides are, it's messy and it collects dust, abrasive dirt, and debris like a magnet. Grease is best used on parts where the mess is a non-issue and routine access is difficult, such as trigger assemblies and internal bolt parts. It's also just the ticket to ensure threaded parts such as choke tubes, muzzle brakes, and muzzle-loader nipples and breech plugs don't corrode and seize up.

Lubricants should be applied very sparingly. Nine-hundred-and-ninety-nine folks out of a thousand way overdo it. Too much lubricant can capture dirt and debris that can then find its way in between moving parts, causing wear and even jamming. It also greatly compounds the gumming problem. One common but ill-fated practice is to take a can of WD-40 type spray and hose down the action, directing the spray through every orifice and crack leading to the interior. Never, ever do that. Not only will juice seep out of the action for days, in time things will become so gummed up in there it will require a gunsmith to completely disassemble the firearm and clean it.

The whole purpose of lubricants is to reduce the friction where moving parts rub together. That's the only place we want it, between those parts. Since the parts are actually touching (or will be sometime during the action cycle) there's not much room left for lubricant so we don't need a bucketful. Just a very thin film directly where the parts touch is all we want. The one exception is when applying grease to threaded parts to aid future removal. In this case, goober the threads all up, using your fingers or a cotton swab to work it down into both the male and female threads. Once assembled, wipe off all the excess that squeezes out.

RUST PREVENTIVES

It's an inevitable fact of life: metal corrodes. Given enough time or extreme conditions, even stainless steel rusts. While rust on a gun's exterior is mostly just a cosmetic annoyance, on critical parts or inside a bore it can ruin the gun. Rust is the equivalent of cancer to a gun. Once it gets a firm hold little can be done about it. We can clean some off the surface but underneath it just keeps growing and growing, forever eating its way down into the metal. The only solution is extreme surgery, meaning part replacement or a complete refinishing job. As with cancer, prevention is much more effective than cure.

Rust is caused either by moisture, corrosive salts, or both in contact with the metal. The most common source of salts is from fingerprints. Black powder and Pyrodex are also laden with corrosive salts. Though rarely encountered any more, the priming compound of WWII and earlier military ammo was highly corrosive as well. Moisture can come from various sources. Rain, snow, or a dunk in the marsh are obvious, urgently beckoning us to dry it off. Much sneakier is atmospheric moisture. The air around us always contains some moisture, in many parts of the country a lot. As a gun sits idle in the rack, microscopic quantities of water collect on its surface and the rusting process begins. Also, powder fouling and dust work like a sponge, sucking moisture out of the air and holding it. Storing guns in cases, especially plastic ones that can't breathe, greatly promotes rusting by trapping condensed water on the gun.

The most practical solution for all this is to coat the metal with something that shields it from water and salts and neutralizes their corrosive action. Commercial bluing (as opposed to cold touch-up blues which do nothing for rust prevention) provides some rust protection but not much. The standard practice of wiping down the exterior metal with whatever oil is handy is certainly better than nothing, as is the common silicone rag. However, there are better, longer lasting alternatives on your dealer's shelf.

Typically called rust preventives, they displace existing moisture, neutralize salts, and leave a thin, rust inhibiting coating on metal surfaces. Unlike oils and grease, most rust preventives do not leave an oily film that comes off on your hands and stains clothing. Though oversimplified, there are two basic types of rust

Oil and silicone help prevent rust but specially formulated rust preventives are far better and last longer.

preventives. One type, such as Brownell's Rust Preventive No. 2 and Sheath, evaporates to leave a dry, nearly invisible film. These leave metal parts looking about as they should. The other grouping, represented by products such as Shooter's Choice Rust Prevent and Outers Metal Seal, employ, as well, some form of wax. In my limited testing those including wax seem to provide a more durable, longer-lasting coating, especially under extreme conditions like a typical elk hunt in the rain soaked Cascade Mountains. The wax, however, does leave a noticeable, slightly sticky film that makes bluing look a bit ratty. For short-term storage around the house or guns on display I use the non-wax rust preventives. However, when the rain Gods are stirring or the gun is headed for a lengthy layoff I bring on those with wax.

Chapter 4

SWEEPIN' THE CHIMNEY: BORE CLEANING PROCEDURES

A barrel is a barrel regardless of the type of action it is hung on. Whether rifled or smooth, long or short, the general cleaning procedures are the same so in this chapter we'll cover bore cleaning generically. However, I'll preface this by saying there's more to keeping a gun happy than just knocking the cooties out of the barrel. There are other areas needing regular cleaning, some areas that only need occasional attention, and places even the fearless dare not go. There we must get into more detail so following this one are chapters devoted to each action type. Each starts with routine action cleaning and maintenance after a day afield or at the range. The final portion of each chapter details advanced cleaning and maintenance procedures for special situations such as long-term storage or preparing for a critical hunt or match. This usually requires disassembling the gun further than casual shooters normally do. It would take a full set of oversize books to detail each and every make and model of gun so we must deal in generalities. Thus, I strongly suggest you have at hand a guide such as

The Gun Digest Book of Firearms Disassembly/Assembly or an exploded illustration of your particular gun. Also, carefully note every step of disassembly as you go, preferably in writing and drawings. Simply reverse the process to get back to a whole gun. If you suspect you might be getting in over your head, quit and take the gun to a gunsmith. They need to eat, too, you know.

Much has been written about the importance of a clean bore for utmost accuracy. Here I'm going to paddle my canoe upstream and blow out just about everything you have read and heard about clean bores and accuracy. Accuracy is a fickle thing. Some guns are inherently tack drivers, others struggle to make a decent showing, and a few are downright embarrassing. There are many, many factors in the accuracy equation and somewhere in there falls barrel cleanliness. Just where depends on the individual gun.

One day I was at lunch with Eric Weeldryer and this subject came up. Eric owns the On Target gun shop in Kalamazoo, Michigan. At the time he also happened to be *numero uno* on the U.S. Shooting Team and twelve-time National Champion. From his considerable experience he is of the opinion that a gun with a quality barrel that has been "settled in" with a couple of fouling shots will shoot very consistently for many, many rounds thereafter with no cleaning. To support his observations he pointed out that Eley, which is the undisputed manufacturing king of target ammunition, never cleans their test barrels. In part, I would have to agree. During law enforcement combat-training sessions I have shot upwards of a thousand rounds through my Smith & Wesson wheel gun between cleanings and noticed no decline in accuracy. I've also been on lucrative ground squirrel hunts with my tricked out, bull-barreled Ruger 10-22 and shot several hundred ground squirrels at considerable range without a thought towards cleaning her.

That said, though, I've also seen many guns that display a distinct accuracy pattern. My long time buddy, a Ruger M-77,

.22-250 Varminter is the consummate representative. After the obligatory fouling shot she'll shoot her best, most consistent groups—nine-sixteenths-of-an-inch for five shots at one hundred yards to be specific—over the next fifteen shots. Then Katy bar the door, she goes to hell in a hand basket. Frankly, I don't know the cause for this, maybe a rough bore or perhaps just the gun god's will. That's okay, though. Unless you're in a competition match where you can't call time out for a cleaning session that's not a big deal. When accuracy starts to go south give her a good cleaning and you're driving tacks again.

Of course, so far we've only looked at bore cleaning from an accuracy perspective. No knowledgeable shooter will argue that guns don't need cleaning at day's end. With the advent of smokeless powder and non-corrosive priming, along came the notion that cleaning soon after shooting was no longer as important. So what if the crud sits in there a day, week, month, or even a year? What does it hurt? First off, powder residue and even copper and lead wash is much easier to remove when it's fresh. The quicker we get to it the less time we must spend scrubbin' and the less need for aggressive solvents. It's easier on our self and the gun.

More importantly, even though not corrosive in itself, gunk in the bore collects and holds atmospheric moisture. With the exception of the chrome plating used on some shotgun bores, there is no rust deterring finish inside a barrel. It's just plain old raw steel. As we've said, even stainless steel can rust. And, of course, any rust preventive or protective oil that may have been present was fried into oblivion with the first shot. As the uncleaned gun sits, the residue continuously absorbs moisture, holding it against the bare metal of the bore. Rust soon forms and happily eats away at the steel unnoticed like a mouse in a cracker barrel.

The same cleaning principles apply to all barrels. The only difference from one gun to another is the type of fouling present, which may dictate using a different type of bore solvent, such as a lead, copper, or plastic remover. Following is the standard techniques used to clean the bore of any rifle, handgun, or shotgun barrel.

BORE-BRUSH USE

The bore brush, whether bronze or synthetic, is our basic tool for aggressive cleaning. The bristles scrub away tenacious fouling and nothing works better to reach into the tight corners of the rifling. It's imperative that the brush is properly sized for the given caliber because it's the tips of the bristles that provide the scouring action. If too large, the bristles are pushed back as the brush enters the bore, leaving only the sides of the bristles in contact with the metal. Not much scrubbing power there. Obviously, if too small, the bristles don't exert enough pressure against the barrel walls to dig into the residue effectively. Likewise, when a brush starts to become disfigured and worn, discard it. They're not that expensive.

Brushes are always used in conjunction with bore solvent. As previously mentioned, don't dip the brush into a bottle of solvent. The solvent must be kept clear and free of grime so we can judge cleaning progress by the fouling coloration left on the patch. Some solvent can be transferred to a smaller container for dipping or the brush can be held over a wastebasket and a small amount of solvent carefully poured onto the brush. Easiest is to use an aerosol solvent which can be either sprayed on the brush or directly into the bore. (Again, be sure to dispose of excess solvent properly to prevent pollution and fire hazards.)

When running the brush through the bore, always make a complete pass, allowing the brush to exit the bore completely. That allows the bristles to realign properly for the next pass in the opposite direction. If you change directions with the brush in the bore the bristles may kink, reducing their effectiveness and shortening the life of the brush. Making complete passes also ensures the entire bore receives proper attention. It's natural, in our subconscious, to tread lightly or even forsake the area near the muzzle and in front of the chamber because of all we've heard about rifling damage at these areas. If you're using a bore guide, as you should, it's a non-issue. Be forewarned, as the brush exits the bore at the muzzle it will likely spray solvent several feet. Place a large waste basket under the muzzle and clear away anything in the vicinity such as other guns or clothing that you would prefer not to be misted with solvent.

USING THE JAG AND PATCH

The jag and patch are used to clear away loose residue and solvent from the bore and to apply oil or rust preventive. A patch also provides some scrubbing action. To work properly the patch must fit snugly in the bore but not so tight you have to muscle it through. That means the jag must be just the right size. Typically, a jag of the given caliber with a standard commercial patch works well. However, if need be, some leeway can be had by using a thicker or thinner patch or multiple patches.

In use, the solvent (or oil) is applied to the patch and the patch draped over the jag. Once inserted into the bore the patch is formed tightly to the jag and the rod can be worked back and forth in the bore without the patch coming off. Once the patch/jag exits the bore, however, the patch has the annoying propensity of falling off. When working from the breech end, I place my fingertip over the muzzle as a stop. If you must work from the muzzle end, mark the cleaning rod with a strip of tape to indicate when the tip of the jag just begins to exit the bore into the chamber. If a patch does fall off onto the floor, discard it rather than risk introducing grit into the bore.

CAUTIONS

Most potential hazards in gun cleaning come from the solvents used. Obviously, commercial bore solvents are relatively safe to use or Uncle Sam wouldn't allow them on the open market. However, that doesn't mean they are idiot proof. Before using any solvent, read the instructions on the label and take them seriously. Most of the more aggressive solvents are pretty powerful stuff and may require special precautions and procedures. Most of us tend to be pretty lackadaisical about label warnings, thinking, "Hey, it's sold over the counter so it can't be that bad. The manufacturer's just covering his butt, right?" Well, think what you want, but I don't figure any one trying to sell a product would put a bunch of scary stuff on the label if it didn't have some merit. As has been noted before, play it safe and wear the recommended protective clothing, provide plenty of ventilation, and avoid prolonged breathing of the fumes.

Also note, some of them caution not to leave the chemical standing in the bore more than some given length of time. Heed that, too. And as cautioned in the solvent section, some solvents can damage stock finishes, both varnished wood and painted synthetics. Try your best not to get it on the stock and if some does, remove it immediately.

BASIC BORE CLEANING PROCEDURES

Whether you're working with just the barrel or a fully assembled gun, secure it in a vise with padded jaws, gun cradle, or similar fixture so you're not wrestling with it and both hands are free. When working with an entire gun, be sure the barrel is tipped just slightly downward so any excess solvent runs out the muzzle rather than back into the action. Be sure you're using an appropriate bore guide.

With barrels accessible from the rear, pointing the muzzle toward a light helps detailed inspection of the bore for fouling, rust, and wear.

The basic cleaning process is the same regardless of firearm type. The first step is to get the worst of the powder residue cleared away. Since this is quite easily removed, we'll use a jag and patches saturated with all-purpose bore solvent. Saturate a patch with solvent and run it through the bore a dozen times or so. Discard that patch and repeat the process. This removes most of the loose stuff which helps keep the brush from getting overly gunked up.

Now switch to the bore brush. Using the plastic "straw" nozzle extension, spray a modest shot of solvent into the bore (or saturate the brush with solvent) and run the brush back and forth full length about two dozen times. Switch back to the patch/jag and run a dry patch through to clean out the crud. Follow that

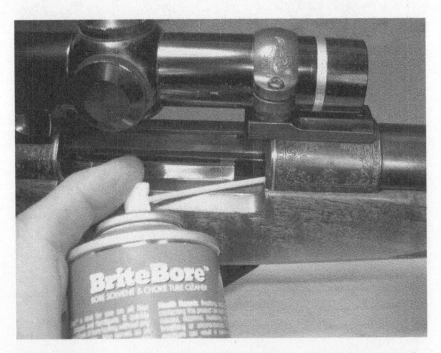

Dipping bore brushes into bottled solvents contaminates the solvent. The author prefers aerosol bore solvents that can be sprayed on a brush or directly into the bore.

with a clean, solvent-soaked patch. Likely the patch discoloring will be mostly black. That's the powder fouling. Keep working back and forth in this same fashion between the brush and patches. Gradually the patch discoloring will turn to lighter shades of gray, possibly mixed with blue or green hues if bullet jacket fouling is present. Repeat this process until, ideally, the patch comes out clean as a whistle.

Note I said ideally. In real life it's not always this simple. If the shooting session was long or you haven't been diligent with regular cleaning there will likely be obstinate bullet jacket, lead or plastic residue remaining long after the powder fouling is gone. Again, the copper bullet residue will show up blue or green on the patch. Lead residue will be gray. Plastic wad or sabot fouling is colorless but can be seen on the barrel walls with close visual inspection. This fouling can be so persistent that it seems there's no end to it. This is where the specialty solvents formulated for copper, lead, or plastic removal earn their keep. Perhaps I should reiterate here that with copper solvent, use nylon bore brushes for the solvent makes no distinction between copper fouling and bronze brush bristles. It eats them both with equal glee.

The chamber is often overlooked in the cleaning/rust preventing process. Because of this it is one of the most common areas on the whole gun to rust. If cleaning from the breech end you can simply use the bore brush and jag. With bottle necked cartridges they will be severely undersize but just work them back and forth all the way around with slight sideways pressure. If the chamber is inaccessible from the breech a chamber brush for the correct cartridge will be necessary. You seldom see these in local gun shops so you'll probably have to order them from a brush manufacturer or gunsmith-supply firm. Because they are compressed so severely in the bore they don't last long, so order several. Push it all the way through the bore into the chamber then work it back and forth while rotating the rod. A patch can be wrapped around the brush to remove solvent and crud and apply rust preventive.

After the bore and chamber are clean they should be protected with some sort of rust preventive. If I'm going to be shooting the gun again in the next few days I just leave a very thin film of all-purpose bore solvent on them. These have enough petroleum content for light rust prevention duty. If the gun will be sitting idle some undetermined length of time it's better to give the bore and chamber a good coat of rust preventive. If it's going to be a long, long time before the gun will see duty again, a heavy coat of grease is the best assurance against rust. Imprint in your brain, though, that these materials must be cleaned from the bore before the gun is shot. Failure to do so may cause potentially disastrous pressure extremes. Put a reminder note in the action to be sure it is not forgotten by yourself or others. Also, while the rust preventive is out, give the external metal surfaces a good wipe down.

That's the general bore cleaning procedure for all types of guns. Now we'll go into the specifics of a routine cleaning session with the various types of firearms.

Chapter 5

CLEANING THE BOLT ACTION

ROUTINE CLEANING

Start by removing the bolt and magazine clip if so equipped. If the magazine is the hinged floorplate type, pop it open. For fixed magazines stuff a paper towel in from the top to catch excessive solvent. If scoped, cover the lenses to ensure no solvent gets on them. Now's a good time to consider the effect bore solvent may have on your stock finish. The outer surface of a synthetic stock may be the stock material itself or it may be painted. Either way it is quite tolerant of standard bore solvents, as are most modern wood-stock finishes. On the other hand, the aggressive solvents may soften these finishes if left in contact too long. If we're careful and immediately remove any solvent that happens to get on the stock we should be okay. Not so with the oil finishes typically used on high grade custom stocks and some antique arms, though. Most bore solvents will eat into oil finishes faster than you can scratch an itch. If you suspect an oil finish be ultra careful with the solvent. You may even want to remove the barreled action from the stock, though that will require the gun be sighted in again.

Secure the gun in the vise or other holding fixture with the muzzle angling just slightly downward to prevent solvent from running out of the bore and into the action. Working from the breech, clean the bore as described in the bore cleaning chapter. Don't forget the bore guide.

After the bore is cleaned and protected with some form of rust preventive, clean the external bolt surfaces with a rag and bore solvent. This removes old lubricant that may be gumming up as well as any grit or other foreign matter. Don't forget the bolt face. Be careful not to get solvent inside the bolt body as this may displace the lubricant on the firing pin, spring, and other moving parts stashed away in there.

Since this is just a routine cleaning we won't strip the bolt down to its undies but we should give some attention to the extractor and, if present, the ejector button. In reality, if the gun is frequently cleaned this only needs doing every third or fourth cleaning but it's a good habit to get into. If the gun has a Mauser-style

While cleaning, always inspect critical parts such as the cocking lug for wear or damage.

extractor (a flat strip of steel running part way back along the bolt body), rotate the extractor to access the areas of the bolt body underneath it. Use a toothbrush to scrub out the narrow groove at the bolt nose in which the extractor runs. You'll note the extractor is attached to the bolt with a steel band, called the extractor collar, running in a channel in the bolt body. We don't want to chance any build up of material under there so we'll switch to an evaporating degreaser such as Birchwood Casey Gun Scrubber or Hoppe's Cleaner/Degreaser instead of bore solvent for cleaning. Apply the degreaser along the edges of the collar so it runs down into the groove. Rotate the extractor back and forth to work the degreaser underneath the collar, wiping off the dirty excess as it seeps back out. Keep working degreaser underneath the collar until no dirty residue surfaces and the degreaser remains clear.

For guns with Sako style extractors (a small, spring tensioned hook at the bolt nose), work evaporating degreaser under the extractor by moving it back and forth. Again, continue until the degreaser seeping out runs clear. Some models such as the Remington 700 and Ruger 77 have a button ejector in the bolt face. Do the same here, working evaporating degreaser down around the button by pushing the button in and out. Use a brass or aluminum rod to work the ejector button as steel may scratch or even deform the ejector tip over time. Continue working degreaser in and out until it runs clear.

Apply a liquid lubricant of your choice under the extractor collar (or behind the extractor hook) and ejector button in the same fashion as the degreaser, working it in by moving the parts. Continue working the parts and wiping off the excess oil that seeps out until no more oil appears. Apply oil to a small rag and very lightly lube the bolt body, leaving only a very thin film. You can oil the face of the cocking lug that contacts the trigger, but wipe it all back off. Excess oil here can screw up proper contact and resistance. Also check the leading edge of the cocking lug for wear. The edge should be sharp with no appreciable rounding. If this appears suspect, a trip to the gunsmith is in order because this could cause an accidental discharge.

Using evaporating degreaser and a toothbrush, rags, and cotton tipped swabs, clean the inside of the action, paying special attention to areas that contact the bolt. Go light with the degreaser to ensure it doesn't run down into the stock inletting or trigger assembly. Try your best to keep it off the stock finish. Should some get on the stock, remove it immediately. Treat hard-to-access parts like a Mauser-style bolt release the same as the extractor, working degreaser in by working the part back and forth and removing what seeps out. Lightly lube the interior action and moving parts with your lubricant of choice.

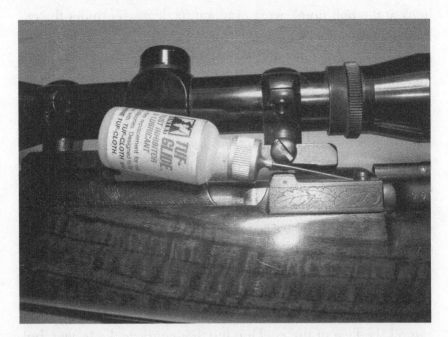

The bolt release should be cleaned and re-lubed regularly to keep it functioning smoothly and prevent rust.

As long as Ol' Bess is in hand, check that the action screws, scope ring, and sight screws are all tight and that there is no noticeable stock damage. Inspect the receiver, bolt handle, and trigger for cracks. It's quite unusual for modern receivers to crack but older rifles, particularly military Springfields, Enfields, and to a lesser degree Mausers, sometimes crack at the front receiver ring. Regardless of make and era, take a good look at the front and rear receiver rings and the action walls between them. Bolt handles, particularly with Remingtons which are soldered on rather than an integral part of the bolt body, can break. This usually occurs close to the base but can happen anywhere along its length. A trigger is more likely to bend than break but give it a look, too. Knock the snakes and spiders out of the magazine box, wipe down all the exposed metal surfaces with your preferred rust preventive, and call it a day.

ADVANCED CLEANING

While a general cleaning is fine for everyday use, occasionally Ol' Thunder Thumper should receive a complete physical. This may be when we're hangin' her up for the winter or perhaps in preparation for a special hunt or critical match where it must function flawlessly. Not only will we clean, lube, and rust-proof everything, we'll inspect for damage and wear. I remind you to use properly fitting screwdrivers as detailed in the tool section. For this example we'll use a typical Mauser-style action as representative of Remingtons, Rugers, Winchesters, and most other common centerfire bolt actions. With just a little imagination it will suffice for nearly all bolt guns, including shotguns and .22's.

Remove the scope rings, scope, and scope mount base. Take out the bolt, remove the action screws, and pull the barreled action out of the stock. If it doesn't come out easily, *don't pry or exert excessive force on the barrel or forend*. Reinstall the action screws but leave them a couple turns short of full seating. Use a plastic hammer to tap on the screw heads, alternating back and forth between them. Start lightly and advance to harder blows as necessary. With luck, that will break the action loose to where it can be rocked back and forth while exerting upward pressure to walk the action out of the stock.

If nothing budges with the screw tapping, place a bath towel on the bench top and grasp the gun firmly by the buttstock and forend as if you were hip shooting. Position the barrel a half foot or so above and parallel to the bench top and lightly whack the full length of the barrel from forend to muzzle on the bench. The barrel must hit the bench top evenly or you risk bending it. Start with a relatively light whack and get meaner as needed, up to a point, of course. That will do the trick 99 percent of the time. If that fails, likely the action was glued into the stock during glass bedding, intentionally or otherwise. Put the gun in the freezer overnight to shrink the metal and glass and try the bench-whack technique again. That's your last chance at benign removal. If that fails, it's time to give up.

If for some reason you must get the action out, the very last resort is to take it to a competent gunsmith. You can tell he's competent if he knows the chemical he can inject between action and stock to dissolve the epoxy bedding compound. It's nasty stuff so I'm not going to tell you what it is. We'll leave those hazards to him, that's why he makes the big bucks (yeah, right). This process will salvage a wooden stock, though it will likely require refinishing. If the stock is synthetic the dissolving chemical will destroy the stock right along with the epoxy bedding.

So . . . back to business. With the action out of the stock, remove the trigger-guard assembly. This can be sticky, too. Take care to pull it straight out. Just grabbing the trigger-guard bow and reefing on it levers the whole works forward which can break the wood at the rear tang. If it won't simply pull out, use a hammer and a tool such as a screwdriver for a punch. Work from the top of the stock, going down through the front and rear action screw holes and trigger and magazine mortises to access the bottom of the trigger guard. Go lightly so as not to ding up the guard. If it's this tight you'll likely have to keep alternating back and forth to work the guard out of the stock gradually.

In most cases the magazine follower spring can be removed from the floorplate and follower by sliding it out from under the tabs holding it in place. Before removing, though, note which end of the spring goes with the follower and which with the floorplate. It may not work correctly if assembled backward. Use degreaser to clean the trigger guard and magazine box inside and out, along with the magazine follower and follower spring. Work degreaser down into the floorplate latch and hinge pin, if present, as previously described for the extractor and ejector on the bolt. Do likewise with a light coat of lubricant. Finish up with a good coat of rust preventive to all surfaces and reassemble the magazine spring and follower.

Now and then we need to get into the bolt's innards to change old, tired grease and just make sure things are hunky-dory in general. Or, if you're going after polar bear on pack ice you may want to remove all lubricant, which can thicken in subzero temperatures, from inside the bolt. Disassemble the bolt according to instructions for your particular model. This typically involves holding the cocking lug to the rear while the bolt sleeve/striker assembly is unscrewed from the rear of the bolt. The bolt sleeve is under very strong tension from the mainspring so it usually requires the aid of a padded vise to hold the bolt body while you engage in combat with it. The bolt sleeve/striker assembly is then disassembled as per prescribed methods for your gun.

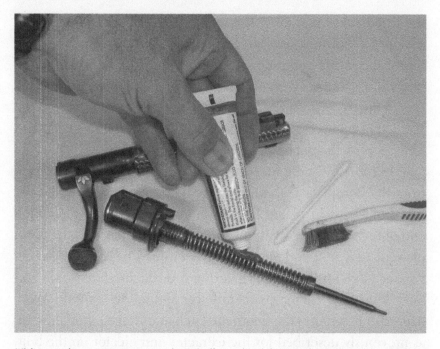

With normal temperatures grease is typically used to lubricate the striker and mainspring as it maintains its properties and stays put better than oil. For extreme, sub-zero temperatures replace the grease with a dry lubricant or even nothing at all.

The Remington-style button ejector is removed from the bolt by drifting out its retaining pin. This is usually a roll pin so be sure to use the proper sized punch to keep from deforming it. Don't completely remove the pin, just drive it out far enough to release the part. The general rule is to push pins out from left to right. It doesn't always matter but it's a good habit to develop. These parts are under moderate spring tension so control the part as the pin is removed so it won't be launched into orbit, never to be seen again. I don't advise removing Mauser-style extractors unless there's something wrong. It's a beast to do and there's a chance the collar will break or bend out of shape.

Thoroughly clean all parts with evaporating degreaser. Use cotton-tipped swabs, brushes, and whatever else works to clean all the nooks, crannies, holes, and crevices in the bolt body. Don't forget inside the bolt body where old grease may be caked on.

Choosing lubricants for the various parts depends on what the gun will be used for. Under normal conditions I prefer a quality grease for lubricating the striker and mainspring. It stays put better than oil and tends to replenish itself on contact areas as needed. As the grease is shielded by the bolt body, collecting debris isn't the issue that it is on more exposed areas. However, if extreme cold conditions are anticipated I would go with a thinner, dry-type lubricant such as Dri-Slide or Tuf-Glide applied sparingly. These same drying lubricants also

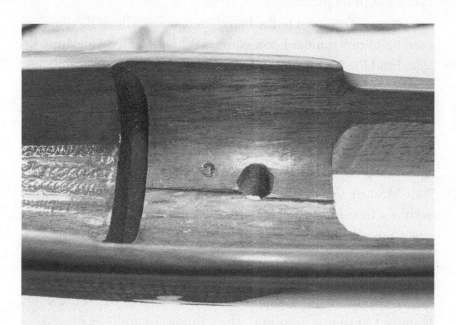

Anytime the stock is removed inspect for cracks not visible from the outside. The area behind the recoil lug is especially susceptible to cracking with hard-kicking magnums.

work well on parts such as extractors and ejectors. The downside is that they seem to get gummy over time quicker than oils. Reassemble the bolt, wipe down all the surfaces with rust preventive, and set it aside.

Next we'll give the stock a thorough inspection. Remove any oil, grease, or other crud from the inletting with a dry rag and/or cotton-tipped swabs. In the case of wooden stocks these chemicals can soften the wood. Look for cracks, paying special attention to the area directly behind the recoil lug and rear-action tang. Should you find a crack it's time to support your local gunsmith for it will only get worse. If a wood stock, check all internal areas top and bottom for bare wood. If so, apply a quality sealer to these areas. Use thin coats, allowing them to dry between applications, to prevent excessive build-up that may cause assembly problems.

Now we're down to the barrel and action. Clean the bore according to our standard procedures. When it's nice and shiny inside, hold the barrel up to a light and closely inspect the area just in front of the chamber. That's where the gas temperatures are the highest which, over time, erodes the steel. If the metal has a scaly appearance, called "alligatoring," and you're sure it's not rust, powder, or bullet fouling, that barrel has pretty much had it. Keep that little piece of trivia in mind when buying a used rifle, too.

Most modern bolt guns have all the trigger parts contained within a housing. Mucking around with this trigger assembly is tricky business and it's best just to leave this alone. Even adjusting adjustable triggers is best left to the pros. The adjustments must remain within certain limits and have to be done in just the right order. If not, the gun may accidentally discharge when the safety is moved to the off position, when the bolt handle is moved, or even when the gun receives a jolt. Take this warning seriously. I do, having personally seen several instances of this, one involving bloodletting.

On most of these trigger assemblies the safety lever is attached to the outer frame with a "C" clip. Usually the lever can be sufficiently cleaned and lubed without removing it but if you're compelled to take it off it's easily done by removing the clip. There is usually a spring and tiny detent ball underneath the safety lever. Take care not to lose those.

In the case of simple military-type triggers there's not much that needs to be done. Clean any debris and old lubricant away and re-oil is about it. If it has a removable trigger shoe, make sure its retaining screw is tight.

General action cleaning has been previously detailed but there are a couple areas that could use further attention. Now and then we should clean inside the front receiver ring behind the barrel. This area is recessed to accommodate the bolt locking lugs and is a little tricky to reach with normal tools and brushes. Fortunately, most of the gunk in there is only powder fouling and can be easily removed with bore solvent. A section of coat hanger wire with a short bend at the tip is handy for working a small piece of rag around in there.

The bolt stop at the rear of the action can be easily removed for cleaning. Most are attached with either a screw or pin. Remove the assembly, noting the location of the parts for reassembly, clean the parts, apply fresh lubricant, and reassemble.

The gun is now in tip-top shape and ready for reassembly. Be sure to put oil on the pins as you replace them and rust preventive on the screws and other non-friction parts. All except the scope-mount base and ring screws, that is. These we will install with Loc-Tite Threadlocker to ensure they don't work loose, so they must be kept free of oils.

One somewhat critical assembly procedure is installing the barreled action into the stock. Place the action into the stock, ensuring it goes in straight and is fully seated. Install the front action screw first. Thread it all the way in and lightly snug it down. Then place a finger on the back of the action tang and thread the rear screw in. If you feel the tang move, no matter how slightly, as you firmly tighten the rear screw that means the action is being sprung because of improper stock bedding. That adversely affects accuracy and in severe cases can even bind the bolt and scope.

For detailed scope-mounting procedures refer to the accoutrement chapter toward the end of this book.

Chapter 6

CLEANING SEMI-AUTO, PUMP, AND LEVER ACTIONS

ROUTINE CLEANING—RIFLES

With most rifles of these action styles we have an obvious problem. There ain't no way we're going to get a cleaning rod into the bore from the back end. We can either use a Bore Snake or go in from the front with a rod. Of course, if we use a rod we'll use a bore guide. Secure the gun with the muzzle slightly downward to prevent solvent from running into the action. Open the action and stuff a piece of paper towel in to absorb transient solvent. Clean the bore and chamber with the normal procedure.

These action styles don't normally provide easy access to the internals. There's not much else you can do in the way of significant cleaning and oiling without major disassembly. Wipe down all the metal surfaces you can reach with rust preventive and that's it.

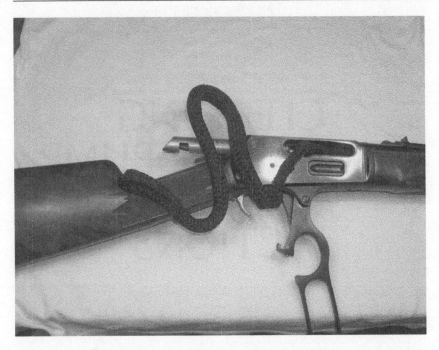

The Bore Snake will not damage the bore as a cleaning rod can and many shooters prefer it for cleaning barrels not accessible from the breech.

ROUTINE CLEANING—SHOTGUNS

If your shotgun is not a takedown model, clean it as previously described for pump and semi-auto rifles. However, most pump and semi-auto shotguns are designed for the barrel to be easily removed. On some models such as the venerable Remington 870, this can be as simple as opening the action, unscrewing the magazine cap, and pulling the barrel forward. Other models may require removing a pin or screws at the front of the magazine tube, rotating the barrel/magazine assembly, removing the forend and gas seals, or some other variation but the procedure isn't usually difficult. When removing the gas piston, piston seal, or steel bushings of semi-automatics, note the way they are facing because they must be replaced in the same manner. If in doubt about any of these procedures, refer to the owner's manual or a firearms disassembly guide such as the previously mentioned *Gun Digest Book of Firearms Assembly/Disassembly*.

With the barrel off, it is easily clamped in to the vise and the bore cleaned with the usual cleaning procedure. If the gun has a choke tube, remove it for separate cleaning. After some scrubbing with solvent, brush, and patches, dry the bore and hold the muzzle toward a light. Look closely down the bore for signs of lead or plastic build up, which usually appears as streaks or slightly dulled, patchy areas. This is usually most prevalent at the forcing cone just forward of the chamber and, if a fixed-choke gun, at the beginning of the choke. If this build up is severe and

The gas ports of gas-operated semi-automatics like this Remington 1100 must be kept clean for the gun to function properly.

defies the bore brush, go to a specialty lead or plastic solvent. If you really get desperate, try a steel Tornado brush (see the bore brush section). Clean the choke tube(s) in a similar fashion.

In the case of gas-operated semi-automatics, clean the gas-port holes on the underside of the barrel with powder solvent and a specially designed gas-port brush. Lacking the brush, an old-fashioned pipe cleaner works just peachy. Clean the steel bushings and rubber "O" ring with solvent, toothbrush, and rag. In the case of recoil-operated semi-autos, simply clean whatever bushings are present.

Clean powder fouling and other residue from the underside of the barrel, the external magazine tube, forend parts, and all other accessible metal surfaces. Very lightly oil moving parts such

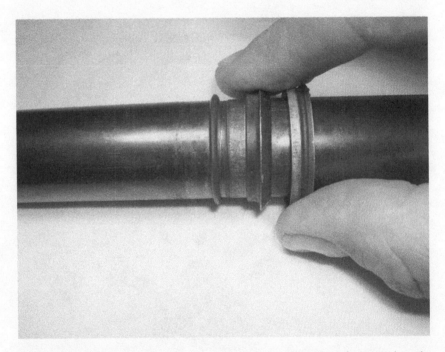

When disassembling semi-automatics note the position and location of parts such as the piston and piston-seal rings. They must be reinstalled in the same order and facing in the same direction.

as the steel bushings and "O" ring and the corresponding surfaces on which they run. For the other areas of metal, give them a good coat of your preferred rust preventive. Reassemble in the exact opposite order you took things apart.

When installing a screw-in choke give both the barrel threads and choke-tube threads a liberal coating of choke-tube grease or other quality gun grease. Don't over-tighten, just snug it down by hand so you can easily remove it in the future. Wipe off the excess grease both inside and out and you're good to go.

ADVANCED CLEANING—RIFLES

This is a place for honest evaluation of our abilities. To get very far beyond the surface of most pump, semi-auto, and lever rifles requires extensive disassembly. Unlike bolt guns, these types of actions can be quite complex. There are a myriad of parts with many working in conjunction with other parts. These usually must be removed and replaced in specific order and some are difficult to access. Some may also require special tools. If you're mechanically inclined, have the right tools, and have specific disassembly/assembly guidelines for your gun, you may elect to venture inside to clean things up and apply new lubricant and rust preventive. If you're of lesser talent leave internal action cleaning to the gunsmith.

There are a few things, though, any of us can and should do now and then. Most of this goes toward the relentless battle against rust. Usually forends are quite easily removed, allowing us to apply fresh rust preventive to areas we can't otherwise reach. In most cases this is simply done by removing a screw or screw/barrel band combination. With the forend off, we can apply rust preventive to the underside of the barrel, front of the action, and, if present, the magazine tube. Don't forget to apply rust preventive to the barrel band and screw when reassembling.

An area that's often overlooked on guns with magazine tubes is inside the tube. To avoid rust and ensure positive cartridge feeding, the magazine spring, follower, and inside tube walls should be cleaned and lubed during periods of extremely high humidity, whenever you suspect rain or snow has gotten into the magazine, or on a general basis at least once a year.

On nearly all makes, these parts can be reached by removing the end cap at the front of the magazine tube. This is usually held in place by a screw(s) or pin. Control the cap as you remove the screw because it is under tension from the magazine spring. With the magazine cap off, the spring and follower are pulled out. Clean everything with evaporating degreaser. A large diameter bore brush and rod is just the ticket for scrubbing the interior of the magazine tube. The spring, follower, and cartridges contact the tube wall, so use a lubricating oil rather than rust preventive throughout. Just a very thin coat, mind you—we don't want to soak our cartridges. Use rust preventive on the end cap and screw(s).

Although this seldom allows you to gain significant access to internal parts, you may want to remove the buttstock on an annual basis. You can then apply rust preventive to the rear of the action and inspect the stock inletting for cracks. Perhaps most importantly, you can apply fresh grease to the threads of the screw(s) that hold the buttstock on. This ensures it's not hopelessly corroding into place, making future removal a nightmare. The buttstock is attached to the action either by a long bolt running lengthwise through the stock or by one or more screws running between the top and bottom action tangs. If in doubt, remove the buttplate. If there's a large hole in the back of the buttstock with a screw or bolt head showing at the bottom, it's attached with a stock bolt. Otherwise, tang screws are holding it.

ADVANCED CLEANING—SHOTGUNS

Gun designers were more user friendly when they developed most pump and semi-auto shotguns. At least some degree of internal action cleaning is well within the scope of all of us. Barrel removal and cleaning were covered earlier so we'll get right to the serious stuff. Our primary concerns inside the receiver are powder residue, dried lubricant, and foreign objects like unburned powder flakes and weed seeds.

Much of the working guts of these guns is usually contained in a single unit we'll call the trigger assembly. This is usually held in place by one or two pins at the lower rear of the receiver. For most common models such as Mossbergs and Remingtons, the action should be cycled to cock the gun, the bolt placed in the closed position and the safety on. Push the pin(s) out and pull

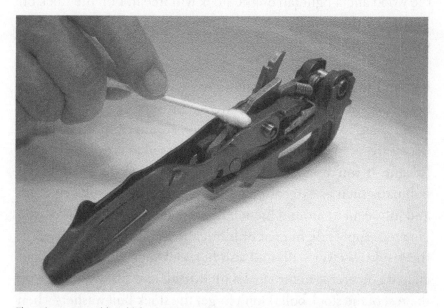

The trigger assembly which contains most of the action parts is easily removed from many pump and semi-auto shotguns such as Remingtons and Mossbergs. This provides sufficient access for cleaning and further disassembly is not recommended.

the trigger assembly downward. Go easy and pay close attention as you remove the trigger assembly because this may allow parts such as the shell stop(s) to fall out.

All those gizmos, springs, and doodads within the trigger assembly can be disassembled but that's just asking for grief. We have enough access to pick out the dead critters, clean things up with bore solvent followed by evaporating degreaser, and to lightly oil all the moving parts. Cotton-tipped swabs, a toothbrush, and rag will pretty much reach everything.

Remove the buttstock from the receiver. In nearly all models it is attached with a stock bolt running lengthwise through the stock. Take off the buttplate (or recoil pad) and unscrew the bolt with a stout, long-shanked screwdriver or socket wrench with extension, whichever the bolt head dictates. A large washer or two should come out with the stock bolt. If not, it's probably stuck to the wood and a light tap on the stock will free it. Pull the stock off straight to the rear. If it proves obstinate whack the comb rearward with the heel of your hand.

With a good disassembly guide it's not difficult to take the bolt and the few other remaining parts out of the receiver. Use bore solvent and whatever swabs, brushes, etc., that seem appropriate to clean the parts and the inside of the receiver. If necessary, evaporating degreaser can be used to dissolve dried lubricant. If you're not adventuresome enough to disassemble the bolt parts such as extractor and firing pin, simply work degreaser and lubricant in around them as described in the bolt action rifle chapter. Apply a light coat of lubricant to all the parts as well as the inside receiver walls and lash her back together. Apply a light coat of gun grease to the stock-bolt threads and rust preventive on the rest of the stock bolt. Don't forget the stock-bolt washers when you reinstall the stock.

Chapter 7

BREAK ACTIONS

GENERAL CLEANING

In the case of side-by-sides, over/unders, and break-open single shots, the barrel(s) are normally easily removed, which alleviates worries of runaway solvent and just makes things easier to deal with in general. In most cases the first step is to remove the forend. Usually this is held on with some form of mechanical latch. Most commonly the release is a lever in the center of the forend or a push button at the tip. On rare occasions the forend is attached with a screw. If there are no levers, buttons, wheels, screws, or other gizmos visible on the forend it should just snap off by pulling on it with moderate force. With the forend off, hold onto the barrel and open the action as you would to load it. In most cases the barrel will just pivot off the hinge pin. In rare instances the barrel opens as normal but then must be lifted upward out of the action. Now we can clamp it dead level in the vise and scrub and grub and slop away to our heart's content.

Once the bore is clean, flop the tube(s) down on the bench and clean what you can reach of the ejector/extractor mechanism with evaporating degreaser. Work the degreaser into inaccessible areas by working the part(s) back and forth, wiping off the goo as it seeps out. A toothbrush, rag, and cotton-tipped swabs all prove useful in this process. Once clean, allow a few minutes for the degreaser to evaporate then lightly oil the parts in the same manner. The various style forend latches can be cleaned and oiled using similar procedures, just be careful not to get solvent, degreaser, or oil on the wood or stock finish.

Now direct your attention to the action. We won't go inside for routine cleaning but there is likely some powder fouling, flakes of powder, and various rubble collected on the action in the vicinity of where the barrel(s) mates. This is all quite easily removed with bore solvent, rag, toothbrush, and cotton swabs. Don't forget the accessible areas of the hinge pin.

There are a number of different styles of locking bars, which is a sliding part in the action that locks the barrel(s) in place. This

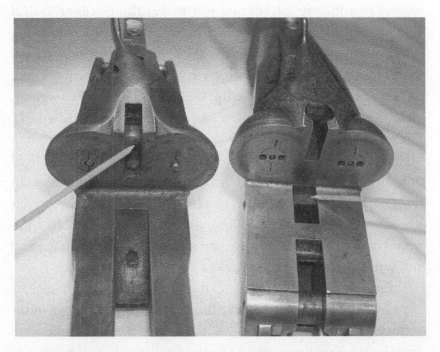

A variety of systems are used to lock the barrels in place but nearly all employ some sort of locking bar (often called "barrel latch") within the action where the barrels mate. This can usually be sufficiently cleaned and lubed without disassembling the action by moving the latch back and forth to work solvent and lubricant in.

bar is located near to where the rear of the barrel mates to the action. It's usually only partly visible in a recessed slot and you should see it move as the top lever is worked. Once opened, the top lever will also lock in place. The release for this will be some form of tab or button in the vicinity of the locking bar, which the barrels activate as they close. To close the top lever, trip this release by pushing on it with a tool such as a pin punch or small screwdriver. Clean and oil the locking bar just as you did the extractor/ejector mechanism, opening and releasing the top lever to move the bar and work in degreaser and lubricant. Finish up the project by applying rust preventive to all exposed metal surfaces, including inside the bore(s), and assembling.

As described in the previous chapter, when installing screw-in chokes apply choke-tube grease or other quality gun grease to both the barrel threads and choke-tube threads. Just hand snug the tubes down for easy removal next time around. Wipe off excess grease inside and out.

ADVANCED CLEANING

Whether shotgun or rifle, over-under, side-by-side or single shot, there are two basic styles of break actions: sidelock and boxlock. The sidelock has removable plates on each side of the receiver to which some of the action parts are attached. A portion of these plates extend beyond the rear of the receiver and are inletted into the stock. The boxlock lacks these lock plates, all the parts being attached to the top and bottom tangs and within the receiver itself. A few models, such as certain Weatherbys, are boxlocks but have false, nonfunctional sideplates to give the appearance of a sidelock, a ruse in the name of aesthetics. As always, before tearing things apart have a disassembly manual for your particular model at hand.

If the gun is a *boxlock*, access the innards by removing the stock. First, cycle the action by opening and closing the barrels.

This cocks the hammers which will allow us to access the firing pins for cleaning once inside. Remove the forend and barrels. Remove the trigger guard by removing its rear tang screw, then gently lift the tang out of the stock and turn the trigger guard counterclockwise to unscrew it from the action.

With some models the stock may be attached by a stock bolt running lengthwise through the stock. Access this by removing the buttplate/recoil pad and use a long, stout screwdriver to unscrew the bolt (note: certain models may require a socket wrench with extension rather than screwdriver). The stock is then pulled off straight to the rear. If it resists, tap the comb stoutly with the heel of your palm. If that fails, clamp the stock in a padded jaw vise and tap the action fences (the lumps

Most of the parts of a boxlock are contained within the receiver. Removal of the stock provides some limited access but disassembly is usually required for serious cleaning. This is a job for the gunsmith.

protruding out each side at the top of the action) with a wood or plastic hammer.

More often the stock is attached by one or two screws running between the bottom and top action tangs. Remove the trigger guard as previously described which exposes a screw that runs up to the top tang. Remove that screw which, in many models, will then allow the stock to be pulled off to the rear. In other cases, the trigger plate must also be removed to release the stock. If so, open the top lever and remove the screw that runs from underneath it and attaches to the trigger plate. Remove the screw at the front of the trigger plate on the underside of the action and pull the trigger plate off.

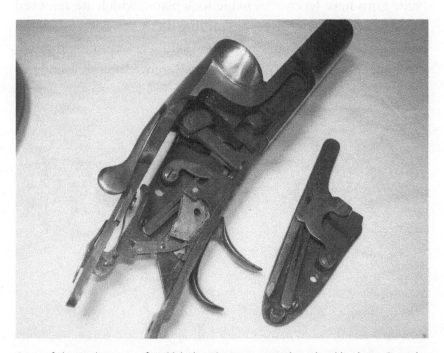

Some of the moving parts of a sidelock action are mounted on the side plates. Removing these plates provides easy access for cleaning many of the action parts. Some parts, however, are contained within the receiver and their disassembly is best left to the gunsmith.

With the stock off we can now get at most everything, at least to a degree. That's as far as I advise going for most parts are pinned in and some are under extremely strong spring pressure which makes them a beast to reinstall. Spray aerosol evaporating degreaser on, around, and under all the parts. Work the degreaser around parts such as the safety mechanism, trigger(s), sears, firing pins, and anything else that moves by working the parts back and forth. Use toothbrush, cotton-tipped swabs, and scraping instruments to remove all the old oil and accumulated gunk. Apply a light coat of your choice of oil or dry lube to all the moving parts, wipe down the metal surfaces with rust preventive, and reassemble.

Sidelocks are treated in a similar manner, the only real difference being the extra step of removing the lock plates. Some high grade guns have lever-detachable lock plates, which are removed by simply turning the lever and pulling them out. More often the lock plates are held in place with a single screw running through one plate and threaded into the other. Remove this screw and run

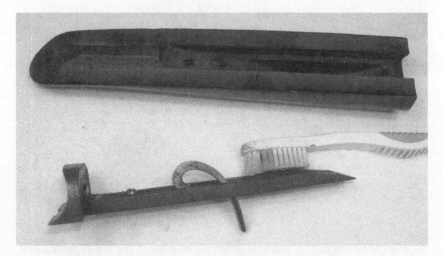

Occasionally the forend iron should be removed for cleaning, the moving parts lubricated, and rust preventive applied to all surfaces. The iron is usually attached by several screws.

a long punch or heavy wire (such as a length of coat hanger) through the screw hole on one side to push the opposite lock plate out. Reverse direction to push the other plate out. From there on disassemble, clean, and oil just as with the boxlock.

Forend latch mechanisms vary greatly but they're not complicated. Typically, removing several obvious screws separates the forend iron from the wood, exposing the latch mechanism. Clean the latch parts and spring, if present, with evaporating degreaser, working it in by moving the parts back and forth. Apply oil in the same manner. Use rust preventive on the remaining metal surfaces inside and out. Before reinstalling the forend iron, check for bare wood in the inletting and at the rear end of the forend. Once again, unfinished wood absorbs oil that can cause the wood to soften. If necessary, apply a coat or two of wood sealer, taking care to not allow build-up that would hamper forend iron fit.

Extractors and ejectors, located on the underside of the barrels, can be disassembled for cleaning and oiling according to disassembly instructions for your model. Truth be known, few problems arise here and degreaser and lube worked in as described in the general cleaning section is usually sufficient.

If the gun sports choke tubes, clean them inside and out with bore solvent and brush all the gunk out of the threads. Apply choke-tube grease or other quality grease to both the tube and barrel threads, screw them in to hand tight, and wipe off excess grease. With the gun completely assembled, give the exposed metal surfaces a wipe down with rust preventive and you're done.

Chapter 8

HANDGUNS

GENERAL CLEANING—REVOLVERS

Routine cleaning of wheel guns tends to be one of the more involved cleaning chores for several reasons. A typical range session with a handgun involves a lot of ammo. Fifteen or twenty rounds with a rifle is a fair amount of shooting but in a handgun that's barely getting warmed up. In addition, typical revolver target ammo utilizes soft lead bullets, meaning a lot of tenacious lead build-up. Also, in addition to the barrel there's anywhere from five to nine holes in the cylinder for all that lead to collect in. Fortunately, with many of the more common models partial disassembly is quite easy, providing easier access to the areas most prone to fouling.

Single-action revolver cylinders can usually be removed by opening the loading gate and setting the hammer at half cock, then depressing a button (for sake of higher education, that's called the "cylinder base-pin latch") at the front of the frame and pulling out the rod (cylinder base pin) that holds the cylinder in place. The cylinder can then be pushed out to the right. That's as far as we care to go for a routine cleaning session. On some makes a screw is used to retain the cylinder base pin rather than the typical spring-loaded button. Removing the screw frees the cylinder base pin.

Firearm designers weren't that nice to us when devising double-action systems. Most of the very early double actions utilize a base pin and latch system similar to single actions. Later on, though, designers exercised their creative talents to come up with a variety of cylinder attachment systems. So you don't look like a dummy, know that with modern double actions the affair that fits into the cylinder and holds the cylinder in the frame is called the "crane." Its function is similar to the single action's base pin, just more complex because of the swing-out cylinder, ejector rod and such.

Many of the earlier double actions were top-break models, meaning a latch at the top rear of the frame is lifted up, allowing the barrel to pivot downward for loading and unloading. With many models, such as those by Smith & Wesson and Iver Johnson, the cylinder is removed by opening the action and, while holding the barrel latch up, unscrewing the cylinder counterclockwise. You may have to exert some rearward pressure on the cylinder to ensure the threads engage. The cylinder of other models like those by Harrington & Richardson is removed by depressing a latch button on the side of the barrel or frame.

With modern Colt, Smith & Wesson, Taurus, and many others the crane is held in place by a screw (S&W, Taurus) or screw and retainer combination (Colt) located on the right side of the frame (viewed from the rear) just in front of the trigger. Some makers such as Charter Arms and New England Firearms stuck the crane screw in the lower front of the frame. Wherever it may be, once the crane screw is removed the cylinder is then swung open and the cylinder/crane assembly pulled forward out of the frame.

To remove the cylinder of a Dan Wesson the barrel and sideplate must first be removed, providing access to the crane retainer that locks the cylinder in place. Rugers are worse yet. You have to

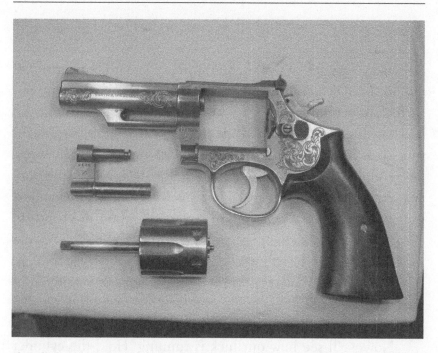

The cylinder and its attaching piece, the crane, are easily removed from Smith & Wesson and Colt revolvers to aid in cleaning. Cylinders of other models such as Ruger and Dan Wesson are more difficult to remove and it may be preferable to leave them in place for routine cleaning.

dissect the whole freakin' gun just to get the cylinder off. In cases like these it's not worth the effort for just a routine cleaning. Leave the cylinder in place and deal with it.

To detail cleaning procedures let's use a common Smith & Wesson K-frame model, which is representative of most modern double actions. For no particular reason I start with the cylinder. Remove the cylinder and slide the crane off. The ejector rod can be removed (reverse threads on S&W) but let's not mess with that for now. It doesn't get very dirty in there so we'll save that for a more serious cleaning session. I will take this opportunity to pass on an ejector rod hint, though. If the ejector rod has loosened and backed out some, the tip can bind on the frame, making opening the cylinder difficult or even impossible. This is a very common malady.

Okay, let's get on with it. Start with a standard bore brush on a short pistol rod. Saturate the brush with solvent and scrub out each chamber, taking a dozen or so passes in each. Recharge the brush with solvent as needed, about every three chambers, to ensure plenty of juice. This loosens up most, if not all, of the powder residue. Chamber diameters are slightly larger than the bore diameter so brush fit is on the loose side. This means we can just use a small piece of paper towel wrapped around the brush to clear the goop out. That's faster and cheaper than switching to a jag and cloth patch. Only use high quality paper towels, though. The cheap brands fall apart, leaving paper strands entangled in the brush bristles. If the gun is exceptionally dirty, or if it has sat a long time before cleaning, repeat this procedure several times.

Now we'll see how our luck is running. Hold the cylinder up, the front aimed toward a light or bright white surface, and closely inspect each chamber. We're looking for lead or bullet-jacket build-up as well as stubborn powder fouling. You'll notice a step in each chamber wall near the front. This is the forcing cone that keeps the bullet aligned as it exits the casing. It's this forcing cone area, and to a lesser degree the area in front of it, that really collects build-up. This is especially true if you're shooting a short version of the cartridge the gun is chambered for, like a .38 Special in a .357 Magnum or a .44 Special in a .44 Magnum. Using lead bullets in this scenario compounds build-up many times over.

If you've been shooting lead bullets it's a sure bet there's still plenty of lead fouling present. Lead build up usually looks like little, irregular scales on the chamber walls, though it may also appear as a rough, slightly darkened area or as thin, lengthwise streaks. Of course, if you only shoot jacketed bullets lead residue is not an issue. Bullet jacket fouling is harder to see than lead. At the forcing cone it usually looks like a slightly off-colored area. Beyond the forcing cone it typically appears as lengthwise streaks.

If in doubt as to the nature of the fouling, run a solvent-saturated patch through the chambers. Bullet jacket fouling will stain a patch blue or green, lead will show up gray. Bullet jacket material will usually succumb to persistent scrubbing with brush and bore solvent, especially if you switch to a more aggressive solvent such as Shooter's Choice. For really obstinate jacket build-up go to a nylon brush and a copper solvent like Hoppe's No. 9 Bench Rest or Shooter's Choice Copper Solvent.

It's the lead build-up that will drive you nuts. That's why a lot of shooters shy away from lead bullets like they were rattlesnakes. As mentioned, the lead builds up in the chamber forcing cone area and puts up an admirable battle against its ousting.

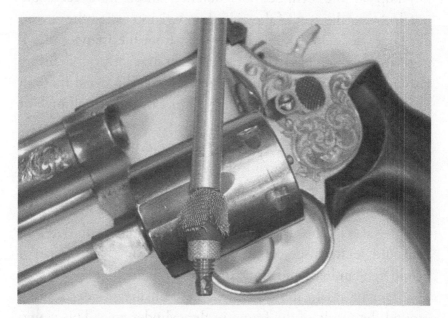

The Lewis Lead Remover works on the order of a jag with a brass screen for a patch. It effectively removes lead from cylinder and bore forcing cones without scratching the metal.

Solvents formulated for lead removal help. One of my favorite tools for dealing with it is the Lewis Lead Remover, which is sort of like a rubber jag utilizing a brass screen for a patch (*see tools section*). The screen digs away at the lead better than a brush without harming the chamber walls.

When the chambers are cleaned to perfection, move on to the outer cylinder. By now most of the exterior powder fouling has been dissolved by solvent that has run out from chamber cleaning so it's mostly just a matter of wiping it off. The front of the cylinder may need a little scrubbing with solvent. I use a toothbrush for this, which cannot harm the bluing. Use a cotton-tipped swab and bore solvent to clean the hole in the front of the cylinder where the crane fits. If need be, pull some cotton off the swab, reducing its size.

Moving back on the cylinder, be sure there's no residue build-up in the cylinder-bolt notches, those little rectangle notches near the rear of the cylinder. A gizmo called the "cylinder bolt," or "cylinder stop," protrudes from the frame and engages in these notches to lock the cylinder in place prior to firing. Extreme build-up of crud in the notches could prevent the bolt from locking the cylinder properly. You can use a toothpick or matchstick to clean these out, if necessary.

Back at the rear of the cylinder is the ejector, the star-shaped affair that fits under the rim of the cartridges. Using the toothbrush and solvent, clear away any residue you can find there. Push on the ejector rod to access the backside of the ejector, which is also toothbrush country. Clean the crane with bore solvent and toothbrush, cotton-tipped swabs, and rag. Wipe the cylinder, chambers, and crane dry and set them aside.

Moving on to the gun itself, note all the powder fouling around the inside of the frame in the cylinder area. This generally comes off quite easily with solvent, toothbrush, and rag. The

Powder residue can build up in cylinder-bolt notches, in extreme cases preventing the bolt from locking the cylinder in place. A small wooden stick can be used as a scraper.

end of a matchstick can scrape the extra-heavy fouling from the inside corners. A quick wipe down with a solvent-soaked rag should take care of the fouling on the outside of the frame and barrel.

Clean the bore like any other bore. After it seems clean, use a bore light (or white patch at the rear of the barrel to reflect light into the bore) and inspect the bore carefully for streaks that indicate lead or jacket fouling. Keep scrubbing until the bore is squeaky clean. Another area prone to lead and jacket build-up is the forcing cone at the rear of the barrel. This aligns the bullet with the bore as it exits the cylinder. With luck, normal barrel cleaning may have gotten it sufficiently. Otherwise it's going to take extra attention. Here, again, the Lewis Lead Remover with its barrel forcing-cone attachment works wonders.

Clean all the solvent from the gun and very lightly lube the ejector rod, crane, and other exposed moving parts. Before putting the gun back together give each chamber a very close inspection inside and out looking for cracks. Cylinder walls are relatively thin and this is more common than you might think. I've encountered several cracked chambers in my time even in quality guns. Also give the top strap a good inspection as cracking here is not unheard of, either. Assemble the gun and give it a final wipe down with rust preventive to complete the task.

GENERAL CLEANING—SEMI-AUTO HANDGUNS

Most semi-autos can be easily field stripped, exposing the areas most prone to fouling for cleaning. Field stripping usually requires a series of steps performed in specific order. Every model is different so refer to the owner's manual or other disassembly guide for your particular brand.

With the gun stripped down to its major components we can now get at most everything that needs cleaning. Clean the bore using our standard bore-cleaning procedures. As with any gun, lead or bullet jacket build-up is heaviest directly in front of the chamber, so pay special attention to this area.

Use bore solvent and a small rag to remove powder fouling and old lubricant from all the exposed metal surfaces. If the gun has been left unattended for some time and petrified fouling and dried lubricant defies the bore cleaner, an evaporating degreaser such as Birchwood Casey Gun Scrubber or Hoppe's Cleaner/Degreaser should do the trick. A toothbrush is handy for getting into the barrel locking lugs and other recesses as well as the interior of the slide. Cotton-tipped swabs are indispensable for reaching down into small, tight areas. The recoil spring can usually be simply wiped clean with rag and solvent. If it's especially nasty it can be left to soak in a shallow pan of solvent while you're cleaning the rest of the gun.

If need be, evaporating degreaser and lubricant can be worked around inaccessible moving parts such as the extractor by applying a small amount at the seam(s) and working the part back and forth. Wipe off the dirty excess as it seeps back out *(see the bolt-action section for more details on this)*.

The magazine seldom requires much attention. At worst there may be a few weed seeds or some pocket lint floating around inside. These can usually be shaken out or picked out through the viewing holes in the sides. I know you wouldn't do it, but if someone in the past made the mistake of hosing down the interior with WD-40 or similar lubricant, that can be removed by a good flushing with evaporating degreaser.

With everything all cleaned up, apply a light coat of lubricant to moving parts, including contact areas of the slide rails, slide, recoil spring and plunger, and so on. Wipe down the rest of the surfaces inside and out with your choice of rust preventive, reassemble the gun and call it good.

My intention is to stick with only sporting arms but here I'm compelled to address defense guns briefly. For handguns carried in a pocket or purse, a good case can be made for using a dry lubricant such as Dri-Slide. This won't collect lint, dust, or other debris that has a special knack for finding a home inside guns. I don't recommend lubricating inside the magazine because it's nearly impossible to get just a thin film. Too much lubricant will eventually turn gummy and muck things up. It could also conceivably wick into the ammo around the primer and bullet, rendering it a dud. If the gun is to be extensively exposed to salt air or high humidity an evaporating rust preventive such as Brownell's Rust Preventive No. 2 can be used. Just apply it as thinly as possible.

If it's a home-defense gun that will be languishing unattended in the night stand or closet corner for months or years *do not use any lubricant.* This goes for all types of guns in this scenario. As I keep harping, every oil and even dry lubricant I've tried will eventually become gummy. Some may hold out longer than others but sooner or later they'll all succumb. This is not the place for a balky or inoperable gun. Just lightly coat all parts with rust preventive.

ADVANCED CLEANING

Because most common handguns are designed to be field stripped for routine cleaning there's not a lot left to do in the way of more in-depth cleaning. With single actions and early double actions it's generally beyond the scope of most amateurs to get into the internal workings. We can take the grips off by removing the screw in the center of the grip. If the grips remain stuck on don't try to pry them off. Turn the screw into the threaded grip as a handle and pull the grip straight off. Simply push the other grip off from the back side. Now we can clean out any chunkies that may have taken up residence in there, inspect the main spring for cracks or damage, and apply rust preventive to all the metal surfaces, including the mainspring and grip screw. A light drop of oil where the mainspring contacts the hammer is a good idea, too. If the back sides of wooden grips are unfinished, apply a couple coats of wood sealer. We should also clean ejector rods by working evaporating degreaser in as previously described for moving parts that are left in place. A light coat of lubricant finishes that task.

We can go a bit further with modern double-action revolvers. Remove the cylinder as described in general cleaning. Now we'll remove the ejector rod and its components for a good cleaning. In many models the ejector rod simply unscrews, though note that Smith & Wessons and some others have reverse threads. Pad the tip of the rod with a piece of leather and use pliers to unscrew it. If it resists unscrewing, load the cylinder with empty cartridge casings (to avoid placing stress on the extractor), secure the rod tip in a padded-jaw vise, and turn the cylinder in the proper direction. Colt ejector rods require a special wrench for removal. Other makes such as various Ruger models all have different procedures for ejector rod removal, some rather complex, so refer to a disassembly guide. Clean all parts of the ejector-rod assembly, cylinder and crane recesses, and other newly exposed areas with evaporating degreaser and lightly lube.

The internals of most double actions can be accessed by removing the sideplate, located on one side or the other of the frame. This will be attached with several screws. With the screws removed, hold the gun cradled in the palm of your hand with the plate side down. The gun should be positioned so when the plate falls off it will drop into your palm. Work over a padded bench top for additional insurance. Tap the frame of the revolver in the grip area with a plastic hammer. The vibration will dislodge the sideplate. Never, under any circumstances, pry on the sideplate as it can be easily bent.

Removal of the sideplate exposes all sorts of gadgets, widgets, and gizmos stashed away in there. Do not disassemble any further as some of the parts may take special tools to reinstall. Remove foreign objects with tweezers, cotton-tipped swabs, or any other tool that seems appropriate. Remove powder residue and old lubricant with bore solvent and evaporating degreaser. Lightly re-lube moving parts, coat the remaining surfaces with rust preventive, and reinstall the plate.

Remove the thumbpiece cylinder latch (that's the button affair you push to open the cylinder) by unscrewing the screw or cap nut that holds it in place. Clean it and the frame surface underneath. Apply a dab of oil to the moving parts and rust preventive to the other surfaces and reattach it. If the gun has adjustable sights, evaporating degreaser can be worked in underneath its parts by adjusting the screws back and forth. Before doing so, note the original settings so you can return there and be reasonably close to sighted in. Add fresh lubricant in the same manner.

Field stripping a *semi-auto* as done for general cleaning gets you to many of the internals. We don't dare go much further than that. Removing the grips safely exposes a few more areas to clean and allows application of rust preventive to that area of the frame. Adjustable sights can be cleaned and lubed as described for double actions. If you feel the need for further internal cleaning it's prudent to employ your local gunsmith.

Chapter 9

BLACK POWDER

Whether cartridge gun or muzzle-loader, black-powder guns require our utmost attention. There's no slacking here. Residue from both black powder and the commonly used substitutes, Pyrodex and Triple Seven, is extremely corrosive and will cause rust to begin forming within hours. Don't think stainless steel is immune, either. Stainless resists corrosion but it's not entirely rustproof.

If at all feasible the barrel should be removed and disassembled for the best possible cleaning. With traditional style muzzle-loaders the barrel is easily removed by driving out the barrel keys located on the forend of the stock. Don't forget to put the

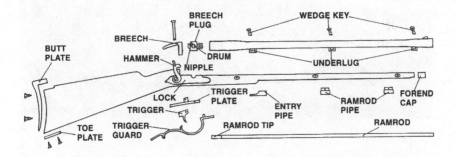

All the parts of a traditional muzzle-loading rifle. Note the narrower middle section of the barrel. This is called a "swamped" barrel which was commonly employed to reduce weight.

hammer in the half-cock position first so it doesn't bind on the nipple (or if flintlock, the frizzen) and break something. Most in-line-action barrels are held in place with a screw at the bottom of the forend. Of course, muzzle-loading-revolver barrels are not easily removed so leave them alone.

Once the barrel is free, the breech plug, drum (if present), and nipple should be removed. This not only allows the barrel to be fully cleaned from stem to stern, the other parts can now be thoroughly cleaned as well. You can't do that well while they're still attached to the barrel. If the breech plug and nipple haven't been removed in a long time they will likely put up a very admirable fight. They really should be removed, cleaned, and the threads greased for future disassembly ease, so you might as well bite the bullet now and get them out.

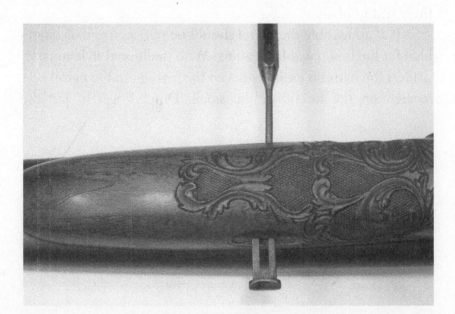

The barrel is easily removed from traditional-style muzzle-loaders by pulling out the barrel keys, which sometimes requires the aid of a punch.

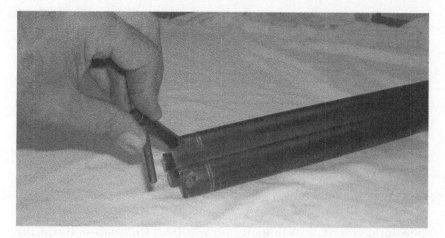

Due to the extreme corrosiveness of black powder and black-powder substitutes, muzzle-loaders should be completely disassembled for every cleaning. Proper-sized nipple and breech-plug wrenches remove these parts without damage.

Make sure the breech-plug and nipple wrenches fit perfectly because you're going to be putting considerable beef to them. If a wrench is at all sloppy it may damage the part and then you do have a real mess. If you're lucky, a few squirts of penetrating liquid such as Liquid Wrench will do the trick. Apply it at the juncture of the parts where it can work into the threads and let it stand, reapplying as needed to keep the area soaked. Occasional light tapping on the parts with a non-marring hammer helps the juice work its way in. Depending on how badly the parts are corroded together, soaking for a few hours or up to a week or more may be needed. I've heard of folks submersing the whole back end of the barrel in a can of kerosene or diesel fuel and letting it soak for a week or two. While certainly effective, this obviously poses a serious fire hazard. Unless conditions allow for the whole works to be stored outside and away from buildings I'd stick with non-flammable solvents. For really obstinate breech plugs an air wrench such as car mechanics use can save the day. The hammering action they provide makes a huge difference. I'm not aware of any commercially available breech plug wrenches designed for air-wrench use so one would likely have to be custom made.

Few things provide such fertile ground for debate as the best black-powder cleaner. Opinions run the gamut from commercial solvents to dish soap to a variety of backwoods witch's brews. The good thing is that, as long as tended to in a timely fashion, black-powder fouling is quite easily removed. At the National Muzzle Loading Championships in Friendship, Indiana, I've noticed hot water and Dawn dish soap to be one of the more popular black-powder cleaners. I'm not sure how critical the soap brand is but that seems to be the one of choice. Whether the popularity of dish soap is more a matter of function or economics I'm not sure, but it certainly works. That's not to say the commercial black-powder solvents don't also work. In fact, most contain agents that not only dissolve the residue, but neutralize the salts that promote rust. This can be an advantage for "quicky" cleaning jobs when the gun is not entirely disassembled.

Personally, when I've had a good shooting session and everything is fare-thee-well sooted up I follow the Friendship experts and use a bucket of screaming hot water and Dawn. That's assuming a rifle or shotgun that can be disassembled right down to its underwear. For revolvers where complete disassembly isn't practical I use a commercial solvent.

For traditional style muzzle-loading rifles and shotguns let's go with a bucket of hot water with a healthy squirt of Dawn dish soap. Of course, the same process pretty much applies to using a commercial cleaner, we just forego the bucket. A word from the wise — this is going to get messy so outdoors, or at the very least over in the nastiest corner of the garage, is the place to do it. Black-powder residue can stain sinks, bathtubs, floors, and countertops like there's no tomorrow. Momma has little patience for that.

Cleaning black powder is messy business and is best done outdoors. Here the author uses hot water and dish soap to clean a percussion shotgun barrel.

Disassemble the gun as described and dunk the breech plug, nipple, and drum (if applicable) into the bucket to soak. Stick the muzzle of the barrel right into the bucket and give the bore a good scrubbing with a bore brush. Use lots of water, even pouring it down the bore with a disposable plastic cup to wash away loose residue. In the case of flintlocks, be sure to clean out the flash hole. If necessary the hole can be cleared with a toothpick but take care not to break it off in the hole. Wash the outside of the barrel, too.

Now is a good time to clean the breech plug, drum, and nipple. In many models the breech plug will have a powder chamber of smaller diameter than the bore. This can usually be sufficiently cleaned with a cotton-tipped swab and solvent. A small-diameter bore brush can be helpful, too. For severe cases you may need to let the parts soak for a while. A toothpick is handy for grubbing around in the nipple flash hole. A nifty trick for the tiny venturi area of the flash hole is to use a single bristle of a common wire brush.

Exchange the dirty, soapy water for fresh rinse water, this time no soap. Make sure it's good and hot, as hot as your paws can stand. This heats the barrel and other metal parts, aiding the drying process by evaporating standing water on the surfaces. Using the same procedure, only this time with a jag and patch, thoroughly rinse the bore, again pouring water inside and out. If the water is noticeably discolored, exchange for fresh and repeat the process until the water remains clear. While the barrel is still hot, dry the bore using clean, dry patches and wipe the water off the outside. Dry the other parts with rag and cotton swabs.

An interesting situation sometimes occurs with black-powder guns that we must avoid. Of course, upon the first shot the bore is coated with corrosive black-powder residue. As shooting progresses this residue can actually become covered over with lead or plastic sabot fouling. If this fouling isn't completely removed during cleaning the trapped powder residue underneath is left to eat happily the bejeebers out of the bore, sight unseen. If the shooting session has been long it's a good idea to finish up with a good scrubbing with lead or plastic wad solvent, whichever is appropriate.

Remove the lock from the stock. Typically this is done by backing out the screw(s) on the left side of the stock opposite the lock. Surely powder residue will be present here both inside and out. For this I use commercial black-powder solvent. Using solvent, rag, cotton swab, and toothbrush, remove the residue from all the accessible surfaces on both sides of the lock.

It's usually not necessary to disassemble the lock for just a routine cleaning. That we'll save for the advanced section. Simply work solvent in, around, and under all the parts by applying a liberal dose of solvent and then cycling the lock a number of times. This is done by firmly holding the lock, cautioning that no body parts are in the vicinity where the hammer falls, and cocking the hammer. Release the hammer by restraining it with your thumb, push up on the sear (the post that protrudes from the lock and contacts the trigger when in place) and ease the hammer down. You must keep pushing upward on the sear while lowering the hammer or it will catch in the half-cock position. Never let the hammer drop without restraint as that puts horrible strain and shock on parts that weren't meant for it. Wash the solvent out of hiding with evaporating degreaser. After the degreaser evaporates work oil into the lock parts just as you did the solvent. Wipe off the excess lube.

If the gun is a flintlock, remove the flint and clean it and the areas it has obscured. The leather is undoubtedly saturated with powder residue, so replace it. The old leather can be washed and reused another time. Clean the frizzen and frizzen spring as you did the other lock parts.

Clean the ramrod with dish soap and water, rinse, and dry. Clean out any debris that may have accumulated in the ramrod channel of the stock. If there is any sign of powder residue in the channel or other areas of inletting of the stock clean that with soap and water. Also clean and apply rust preventive to the ramrod ferrules inside and out as powder residue from the ramrod can accumulate there and cause corrosion.

Inspect the stock for cracks, paying special attention to the area around the lock. If there is any bare wood apply several coats of wood sealer, being sure to not allow build-up that may affect lock fit. After the wood sealer dries, apply rust preventive to all metal surfaces, put her back together and call it good.

If the gun is a modern in-line, the bolt, nipple, and breech plug can be removed and the barrel cleaned with dish soap and hot water as with traditional muzzle-loaders. The breech plug and nipple can be cleaned with water but don't use water on the bolt. If water were to get inside the bolt it would have to be disassembled to dry. Of course, the bore can also be cleaned with commercial black-powder solvent, brush, and jag like a modern bolt rifle. Surely you were using saboted bullets, which virtually all of these guns are designed for. Pay special attention to plastic build-up. Many of these bores tend to be a bit rough and collect plastic extravagantly, trapping corrosive powder residue underneath as previously described. This may warrant using plastic-wad solvent.

If only a few shots were fired and we'll be using the gun again soon we can probably forego disassembling the bolt. Clean the outer surfaces of the bolt with commercial black-powder solvent and lightly oil it. A cotton-tipped swab handles the recessed bolt face. If it appears that powder residue may have gotten inside the bolt body, go ahead and disassemble it for cleaning as described in the owner's manual. Better safe than sorry.

The stock around the breech area may be a little sooted up. Most black-powder solvents are probably okay to use on stocks if they're quickly removed but it makes me nervous. Even with synthetic stocks I prefer to use soap and water. Inspect the stock for cracks or other damage. If there's bare wood anywhere seal it with wood sealer.

Be sure the breech plug and nipple are fully dry, grease the threads (grease, not oil, mind you), apply rust preventive to all the surfaces that will disappear when the gun is reassembled, and put the whole works back together. Give all external surfaces a coat of rust preventive and it's happy hour.

ADVANCED CLEANING

About the only thing left to do for more serious cleaning is to disassemble the lock of traditional muzzle-loaders or the bolt of in-lines. This is a good thing to do on a fairly regular basis just to ensure there's no rust forming in hidden places and so that screws don't become corroded in place.

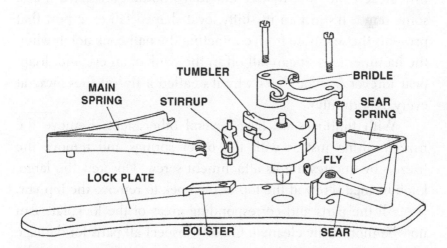

The parts of a typical muzzle-loader lock. The internal parts of flint and percussion locks are the same.

Though a muzzle-loader lock looks complicated it's really quite simple to disassemble *(see diagram for part nomenclature)*. The procedures are similar for both flintlocks and percussion. Remove the mainspring—the large "V" spring that drives the hammer. This is most often held in place by a peg at the rear of the spring fitting into a hole in the lockplate. This is best done with a special spring-compression tool but in a pinch it can be done with pliers. When using pliers pad the jaws with leather. Compress the spring just enough to remove all tension and pull it straight up to remove the retaining peg from its hole. Remove the sear spring in a similar manner, though this is usually held in place with a screw.

Remove the large screw at the base of the hammer (called a "cock" on flintlocks) and pull the hammer off. This can be quite tight and may require some gentle prying. If so, pad both the lockplate and hammer to prevent damage. Some Liquid Wrench may be called for if the screw's corroded in place. Remove the bridle screws and pull the bridle off. This frees the remaining parts. While removing them, keep a sharp eye out for a tiny piece called the fly *(see diagram)*. Some guns have it and some don't. It's just an itty-bitty, oval shaped tab on a post that prevents the sear nose from contacting the half-cock notch when the hammer falls. It can fall off in the wink of an eye and disappear forever (maybe that's why it's called a fly—it flies away at every opportunity).

With flintlocks we have several other steps. Remove the frizzen spring just as with the other springs and remove the frizzen by unscrewing its attachment screw. Unscrew the large, knob-headed screw at the top of the cock to remove the top jaw.

All the parts and corresponding areas of the lockplate can now be thoroughly cleaned. Closely inspect all parts for damage or wear. Look for cracked springs. This most often occurs near the sharp bend at the base of the spring. Check the sear notch

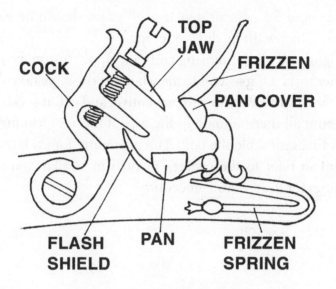

The proper names for flintlock parts.

Modern stainless-steel muzzle-loaders are not immune to black-powder corrosion and must be disassembled for every cleaning. A small-caliber bore brush is useful in cleaning the smaller chamber hole in the breech plug.

and sear nose for wear or damage. All edges should be well defined and sharp with no dings or chips.

Lightly oil all the moving parts and apply rust preventive to the other surfaces, reassemble the whole works, wipe down all exposed metal surfaces with rust preventive, and call it good.

About all there is to do in the way of further cleaning of inlines is to disassemble the bolt. The procedure for each model is different so refer to the owner's manual or similar disassembly guidelines for the specific procedure.

Chapter 10

METAL MAINTENANCE AND REPAIR

The most persistant nemesis firearm owners must deal with is rust. Humidity causes rust, fingerprints cause rust, black powder causes rust, certain leather-tanning chemicals cause rust. It seems everything serves to promote rust. In the early days, gunmakers discovered that applying acid to steel and allowing a certain amount of controlled rusting created a finish that helped to deter rust. That became known as "browning." Sometime later it was discovered that boiling this acid-rust finish in water turned the mundane brown color to black, sometimes with a bluish tint. That was considered quite sexy in most circles. Boiling also improved the durability and rust-resistance of the finish. Hence, bluing was born. To this day a first-rate acid blue is still the most durable, rust-resistant, and attractive form of bluing. Unfortunately, it is a difficult art to master, labor intensive, and agonizingly time consuming, taking up to several weeks. Therefore, we only see it on the most elite, upper-echelon firearms.

Nearly all professional blue jobs today are done by boiling the metal in specially formulated bluing salt solutions. It's a fast, simple process that only takes several hours. The resulting finish is relatively rust resistant and withstands wear quite well. Though we now have other metal finishes far superior in all regards to bluing, for the most part we still insist our guns have a blue finish. It's a steadfast tradition that only recently is showing signs of weakening. Note that I use the term "rust resistant," not rust-proof. Browning and bluing help deter rust to a degree but do not make steel immune. At the slightest opportunity rust will find its way in. Also, stainless steel is only rust resistant. Though it resists rusting far better than regular blued steel, it will rust.

As I keep harping, rust is like cancer with prevention being far more effective than cure. Our best line of defense is to keep all steel parts healthy with liberal and frequent coatings of rust preventive, oil, or grease, depending on the situation. Proper storage is equally important. Large and/or rapid temperature changes can cause condensation to form on the metal, as does high humidity. Damp basements and unheated garages must be avoided at all cost. Store guns in an atmosphere-controlled area of the house where heat and air conditioning keep temperature and humidity constant. It also helps to store guns in an enclosed area such as a cabinet or gun safe. Here a desiccant such as silica gel can be utilized to draw moisture out of the air. Just remember to change it frequently. Better yet are mechanical dehumidifiers designed for use in gun cabinets. Last but not least, go through all your soft gun cases and set aside any that are made of plastic. Bundle these up, including the one your dearest gave you for Christmas, and take them to the trash. These are the most common cause of severe gun rusting because they trap moisture inside and block air circulation. Of course, we need the hard plastic or metal cases for short-term transportation but otherwise all gun cases should be made of a breathable material like leather or cloth. Even with breathable cases, never store guns in them for any length of time. They are for protection during transportation, that's all.

In its early stage, rust is hard or even impossible to see, especially on dark surfaces such as bluing. No doubt you've wiped down a gun that has been in storage and noticed the rag stained light brown. That's microscopic rust particles. Fortunately, you caught it early and the only damage was perhaps a slight lessening of the bluing's ability to block future rust. By the time you can clearly see rust formation some damage to the bluing and surface of the steel has been done. This rust must be somehow removed or neutralized or it will continue to eat into the metal, creating pockmark pits in the steel. The severity of rusting is not determined by how large the rusted area is, but rather how deep into the metal the rust has gone.

RUST REMOVAL

Minor surface rust can be removed with steel wool, which is better than a wire brush as it is less likely to scratch the surrounding bluing or steel. Steel wool is typically graded by a series of zeros, each called an "ought" in steel wool jargon. Steel wool with very course fibers is labeled No. 0 (called "one ought"). Somewhat finer is No. 00 ("two ought"), then No. 000 ("three ought"). The very finest is No. 0000 ("four ought"). Obviously, the coarser the steel wool the more scrubbing power it provides but also the larger and deeper scratches it may leave. On bare steel No. 00 steel wool provides a reasonable compromise between aggressive scrubbing and minimal scratching. If the area is blued, browned, or parkerized use No. 000 steel wool and not too strong with the elbow grease lest you damage the finish. No. 0000 steel wool will cut microscopic surface rust but is too wimpy to accomplish much else in the rust-removal arena.

More severe rusting, meaning deeper metal pitting, requires more than just steel wool. The best solution is to remove completely all the rust pits by grinding and sanding. The problem is that so many parts of a gun are shape or dimension critical that removing any amount of metal is treading in tricky territory. This is best left to a competent professional. He knows where he can go, where not to and when it's best just to replace a part rather than muck with it. Even with non-critical areas such as the outer barrel, action, or frame, sanding is going to trash the adjacent bluing. That leaves bare metal which is highly prone to rusting. Cold touch-up blues do nothing to deter rust so that would mean rebluing the entire gun, an expensive process. Even if the metal is stainless steel, it is something of an art to blend the repair into the overall polish.

A rust-removing gel helps to remove and neutralize severe rust. It removes bluing with equal gusto so it must be confined to the rusted area.

However, you can remove much of the visible rust and curb the rusting process, at least to a degree, yourself. Remove what surface rust you can with No. 00 or No. 000 steel wool. Then use an X-Acto knife to scrape and pick rust carefully from the damaged area. I generally prefer the curved tip blade for scraping while the narrow point of the pointed blade is just the ticket for digging down into the pits. Follow this up with a rust-removing gel such as Naval Jelly or Brownell's Rust & Bluing Remover Gel. Be aware that bluing and browning are forms of rust and these chemicals will attack it in an instant. If the damaged area is small, apply the gel with a toothpick. For larger areas use a cotton-tipped swab. Work the gel down into the pits the best you can and let it stand a while to let it do its business. Carefully

Scraping is one of the best ways to remove surface rust. A small hobby knife is the author's tool of choice.

remove the gel and immediately flush the area with water. For severe pitting several applications are advisable. Thoroughly dry the area (a hair drier is ideal for the job).

If the area was originally blued, apply a cold touch-up blue as per label directions (*detailed coverage on cold blues follows*). It won't be a great color match but at least the area won't shine like a neon sign. Thoroughly dry again and follow up with copious amounts of rust preventive. For this, especially, I like Brownell's Rust Preventive No. 2. The stuff wicks into pits thoroughly. That pretty much stops the rusting action for now. However, the damaged area will forever be susceptible to rusting so it will require regular applications of rust preventive.

BLUING DAMAGE

Bluing is far from bullet proof and we often see it scratched or dinged or simply worn off from routine carrying and use. The resulting bare metal is not only an eyesore, but also opens the door to rust. Unfortunately, the rusting problem can only be cured with a professional reblue job. We can, however, use bluing solutions designed for home use to darken the bare metal to make it less offensive (that's assuming it is standard carbon steel. Stainless steel and other alloys cannot be blued). The easiest and most common method is to use a cold touch-up blue. There are dozens of brands on the market with new ones coming and going all the time. They are very simple to apply, most just being swabbed on, allowed to stand for a minute or two, rinsed off, and then carded with steel wool. Some are available in both liquid and gel consistency. The gel, of course, stays put on rounded or uneven surfaces where the liquid would run off, perhaps affecting adjacent bluing.

All cold touch-up blues have some limitations we should understand. Touch-up blues are for cosmetic purposes only. I've

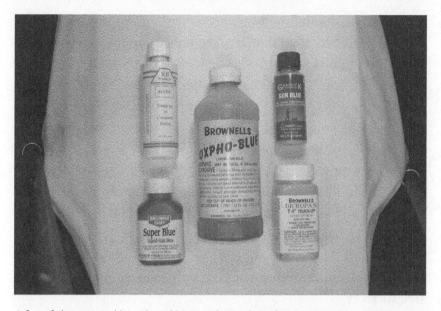

A few of the many cold touch-up blues on the market. They vary in color so experimentation is necessary to find the one most closely matching your gun. Cold blues are for cosmetic purposes only and provide no rust protection.

not found any that provide any amount of rust protection. In fact, I suspect some cold blues may actually promote rust. For instance, I have a sporterized '03 Springfield that I just couldn't find the time to blue. I needed some photos of it for a magazine article and since the publication wasn't rated adult-XXX I couldn't portray it naked so I swabbed the whole thing down with cold blue. Afterward it got rat holed in the rack alongside a completely bare metal rifle also awaiting that "someday" blue job. Both were equally treated with mineral oil, which isn't great for rust protection but doesn't cause bluing problems like more serious oils and rust preventives. It was a hot, muggy, Michigan August and upon checking them a month or so later the cold-blued Springfield was finely freckled all over with rust. The other with bare steel was fine.

Most cold touch-up blues aren't particularly durable, either. When applied to areas that are frequently handled such as floorplates and bolt knobs they soon wear off. No real biggie, of course, for more bluing is easily reapplied. One exception to this is Brownell's Oxpho-Blue. That stuff resists wear like chrome plating. You can scrub on it with steel wool until the cows come home and it only gets happier. That's a good way to test bluing durability. Apply test patches of a number of brands to a piece of scrap steel and go to work on them equally with No. 000 steel wool. It's soon obvious which ones give out and which ones stand and fight. Another nice trait of Oxpho-Blue is it's the only one I'm aware of that will tolerate oil on the steel surface during application. All other blues will take only on absolutely clean, oil-free surfaces.

There's more to a touch-up blue than durability, though. Since its function is mostly cosmetic, it ought to match the color of the surrounding blue. That's the downside of Brownell's Oxpho-Blue. The final finish is a shiny, rather odd gray-black that has little resemblance to typical factory blues. This is where all the various brands come into play. Factory bluing comes in a wide spectrum of shades from deep blue to black, depending on the manufacturer and the chemicals used. Likewise the cold touch-up blues. Trial and error with the various brands of touch-up blues is the only way to find the best match. I've also had some success with mixing cold blues for a better match, though this requires some knowledge of each brand's color propensity. Don't mix the solutions. Apply several coats of one brand that, let's say, leans more toward blue. If it's too blue, then apply another brand that is more of a black shade. Not all the bluing brands are compatible with each other but it's worth a try. The worst that can happen is that the brand used second doesn't take and nothing is gained.

Finally, no matter what the manufacturer claims, cold blues are not suitable for complete gun re-bluing. As previously pointed out, they do not resist rust and most lack durability. It's also next to impossible to get even coloring over large surfaces. A gun finished with cold blue looks like a cross between a leopard and a zebra, with uneven spots and streaks everywhere.

If an entire part is involved, there are alternatives to cold touch-up blues. The easiest is simply to take it to a gunsmith who does hot-salt bluing. He can throw it in the tank along with other stuff and it shouldn't cost an arm and a leg. For the do-it-yourselfer there are blues I'll generically call "Belgian Blue." Belgian Blue was formulated a half century ago by the old Herter's Company. The original firm is long defunct but their Belgian Blue formula survives in other hands. A similar product is Brownell's Dicropan "IM."

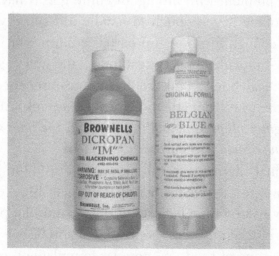

Bluing solutions such as Belgian Blue and Dicropan IM require boiling the parts between coats. They provide a deeper, more durable finish than cold blues but lack the rust prevention of commercial bluing.

These blues fall in between cold touch-up blues and acid-rust bluing, both in ease of application and quality. Application is nearly identical to acid-rust bluing. The bluing is applied in a series of applications, boiling the part(s) in water, and carding off the residue with a special wire carding brush (available from Brownell's) between each application. It may take as few as four or five passes or as many as ten or twelve, depending on the size of the part and the steel involved. The difference between applying Belgian Blue and acid-rust blue is that with acid blue the part must sit for hours or even days between each application. With Belgian Blue it's all done in one continuous process, the parts being boiled immediately after each application of blue. While the durability of Belgian Blue is superior to typical cold touch-up blues, its rust prevention is only marginally better at best, falling far short of acid-rust blue.

Belgian Blue can be used to blue individual parts or an entire gun. Relatively small parts can be boiled in a pan on the stove. The problem with bluing an entire gun is having a tank and heat source large enough to handle it. Even if you have a tank large enough for long gun barrels, a burner or two on the stove doesn't provide enough heat to boil the water aggressively, which is critical. Such a tank requires a pipe burner or something similar running full length underneath the tank. Also, *barrels must be tightly plugged as boiling water on the bare steel of the bore will cause rusting to start within minutes.*

The final alternative is full blown acid-rust bluing. As mentioned above, it is applied similarly to Belgian Blue, except that the lengthy rusting time between coats expands the project into many days instead of several hours. Pilkington Classic American Rust Blue is one of the more popular formulations and is available from Brownell's.

BROWNING

Traditional muzzle-loaders are most often browned rather than blued. Touching up defects or wear of the brown finish is a bit trickier than simply swabbing on cold touch-up blue. Pretty much cornering the market for browning touch-up work is Birchwood Casey's Plum Brown finish. This is applied by heating the part with a propane torch then swabbing on the solution. The metal must be hot enough to make the solution sizzle but take care not to cook the bejeebers out of it. Too much heat can destroy the surrounding browning or even affect the heat treatment of the metal. Too little heat and the finish comes out a shiny copper color. Follow the application instructions to the letter as there are several other pitfalls that can bite you. It can be used to brown large parts as well, but getting the part evenly heated can be difficult. This is sometimes better done with the kitchen oven than a torch.

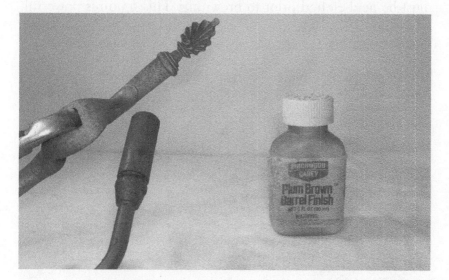

A quick browning job can be had with Birchwood Casey's Plum Brown finish. The parts must be heated quite hot, typically with a propane torch or in the oven.

Another solution for browning entire parts, including barrels, is Laurel Mountain Forge Barrel Brown & Degreaser. This is very similar to acid-rust blue formulas and, in fact, can be used as such by boiling the parts between applications. For browning, the solution is swabbed on, allowed to stand a few hours and then rinsed off with hot tap water and a coarse rag. This process must be repeated up to a dozen times, so it's a long-term project encompassing many days.

While on muzzle-loaders and browning I'll briefly mention treatment of twist-steel shotgun barrels, often erroneously called "Damascus barrels." These were used on all shotguns, both muzzle-loading and breech-loading, until fluid-steel barrels began to make inroads in the 1890's. In their original finish twist-steel barrels display a very attractive swirling or chain-like pattern. If the barrels are sanded and polished clean, then simply re-browned, this pattern is lost. To bring out this pattern the steel must be acid-etched prior to browning. This requires powerful,

The distinctive swirled pattern of a twist-steel barrel.

volatile acids, so it's somewhere no amateur should tread. It's a job for the pros. Bear that in mind when buying a shotgun from the turn-of-the-twentieth-century-era: Barrels refinished to look like safe-to-shoot fluid steel could actually be twist steel, which is best left hanging above the mantel.

FINISHES FOR ALLOYS AND OTHER METALS

There are several other metals besides carbon steel commonly used in firearm manufacture. In the early days various parts were made of brass and German silver to jazz up a gun's sex appeal. Today, many manufacturers use aluminum alloys for parts such as trigger guards and sights or, occasionally, entire guns. Sometimes lead is exposed at soldered joints and, of course, stainless steel and titanium are now in vogue. With the exception of stainless and titanium, these metals readily oxidize so they need some protection to keep from getting all tarnished and nasty. None of them will take bluing so we must turn elsewhere. For non-professionals that means paint. Not hardware-store enamel, mind you, but modern, high-tech formulations, most of which stand up to cleaning solvents and some that rival the durability of bluing. The gunsmith-supply firm Brownell's carries an array of these paints in colors that resemble a variety of gun finishes. They are available in aerosol, brush-on, and even ink-pen form.

For simple cosmetic touch-ups, a one-part epoxy or urethane paint is the easiest to apply. If the part is subject to wear, consider going with a two-part epoxy or urethane as these are more durable. Be sure to follow the mixing directions precisely. If an entire part is to be refinished, perhaps one of the bake-on finishes will provide the best results. These are sprayed on, then the part baked in a regular kitchen oven, which in some magical fashion makes it much more durable than if just air dried. One of the best choices for all around use is baking lacquer. Available in clear and colored, it goes on exceptionally thin yet is very durable. The clear matte version does a very credible job of re-creating the "coin finish" look often seen on double-barrel shot-gun receivers. Baked on epoxies are extremely durable and come in a variety of colors but I've not found it in clear. These will gen-erally have thicker build-up than baking lacquer, which can be an issue when part fit is involved.

The key to success with any paint is to ensure the metal is squeaky clean and free of corrosion before the paint is applied. This is especially critical when coating aluminum as it starts to form mi-croscopic corrosion within seconds after air contact. I always give aluminum a final polishing just before applying the paint. Some of these paints require a special aluminum primer, others don't. The primer is available at the same source as the paint.

STAINLESS STEEL REPAIR

It was once imperative that the metalwork of a fine firearm be blued, or at least look like it was blued. That's why for decades Remington has gone to considerable length and expense to plate the stainless steel barrels of their Model 700 magnum rifles with a dark finish. That has all changed and now it's totally fashionable for a stainless steel firearm to go *au naturel*. Being an old-school curmudgeon I still find it hard to warm up to that look but I must say a natural steel finish allows a lot of latitude for repairing dings and scratches. We can file on it, grind it, sand it, and polish it with little worry about covering up the mess afterwards.

Of course, we don't want to get too carried away with the coarse, scratchy stuff because all deep scratches have to be pol-ished out. For a deep scratch or rust pitting I use the finest-toothed file I can find. A jeweler is a good source for these files. If the blemish is less severe I use No. 220-grit wet-or-dry sandpaper backed by a piece of wood, say a Popsicle stick or wooden dowel. I much prefer wet-or-dry sandpaper (used dry) over the more traditional emery or crocus cloth. Cut the sandpaper into small squares of appropriate size with cheap scissors and wrap it tightly around the wooden backer.

Stainless steel is rarely finished off with a fine polish. That would make it shine like it was chrome plated. Most often manufacturers give it a dull sheen by polishing only down to somewhere around No. 400 grit, give or take a little. This isn't too difficult to match. After the repair is made, polish out any file marks or other deep scratches with No. 220-grit sandpaper. End up sanding only in one direction so all the scratches run the same way. Switch to No. 320-grit and sand in the opposite direction. This makes it easy to tell when all the previous scratches are removed. Examine the scratches closely to see how they compare with those of the rest of the gun. If they seem close, sand in the same direction as the factory polish to see how it blends. If the scratches are still a bit coarse switch to No. 400-grit, ensuring all the previous, deeper scratches are removed. You can also try softening the sandpaper scratches with No. 000 steel wool for a better blend. Depending on how fine a polish the manufacturer applied you may have to go to No. 500-grit paper or finer and perhaps to No. 0000 steel wool but you get the idea. Just make your scratches match the factory's.

The other common stainless steel finish is sand blasting or bead blasting which gives it a frosted look. This makes life a bit tougher. Make the repair and sand out scratches with No. 220-grit paper as previously described. We'll duplicate the frosted look as best we can by laying relatively coarse sandpaper over the repaired area and tapping on the back of the sandpaper with a hammer. Any inexpensive sandpaper will do. You'll have to experiment to determine how coarse the sandpaper should be and how hard to strike with the hammer. For starters we'll err on the fine side so start with No. 180-grit paper. Run the hammer with light, rapid taps while continually moving the sandpaper around to ensure full coverage of dimples. If that's too fine, which it likely is, try No. 120-grit, No. 100-grit, or even No. 80-grit. Obviously, if the No. 180-grit is too coarse, go finer. As with the polishing scratches, the frosting can be softened with No. 000 steel wool. The match will be far from perfect but better than if just left bright.

Chapter 11

STOCK MAINTENANCE AND REPAIR

WOODEN STOCKS

In order to know the best way properly to maintain gunstocks you must have some basic knowledge of stock wood and finishes. Today there are four types of stock woods commonly used in factory gunstock manufacture. In the United States the most common is black walnut. Black walnut grows naturally only in North America and the tree is still quite plentiful. Black walnut is found on nearly all of the middle- and upper-priced, wood-stocked guns made in the U.S. English walnut, also called French, Italian, Turkish, Circassian, or whatever region where it was cut, is the European counterpart of black walnut. The wood itself tends to be a bit lighter in weight, finer grained, and carves better than black walnut. It is the standard stock wood for guns made outside the U.S. English walnut is also commercially grown as a nut crop in orchards all around the globe, including the United States. Even though the wood from these cultivated trees is inferior to wild grown trees, here in the U.S. it still commands such a high price it goes to the custom gunstock market rather than gun manufacturers. Occasionally American manufacturers will go all out and use fancy-figured English walnut on their very high-end models but that is becoming more and more unusual.

On inexpensive, low-end guns where penny pinching is essential, some manufacturers turn to cheaper wood. In the U.S. this is most often birch. Birch is nearly white in color, about like pine, carves poorly, and is not as strong as walnut. It is always stained to more or less resemble walnut but an experienced eye can tell it from across the room. On the other side of the pond, foreign manufacturers similarly cut cost with a wood that I haven't identified but would guess it to be in the mahogany family. It, too, is light in color and must be stained to pull off the walnut ruse. I point this out because it can be difficult to blend a repair of these light-colored woods into the original finish. That we'll get into later.

STOCK FINISHES

In order to maintain and repair stock finishes properly we must have a basic knowledge of the finishes used on gunstocks. From the day someone first lashed a wooden handle onto a gun, boiled linseed oil was the number one stock finish (boiled refers to the refining process, not something the end user does). Linseed oil is extracted from flax seeds and proved to be the best stock finish until well into the nineteenth century. To this day the warm, satiny look of a polished linseed oil finish is unparalleled. Function-wise, however, it has significant drawbacks. Linseed oil takes forever to dry and even after it's cured, high heat and humidity turn it tacky again. Bore solvents dissolve it almost immediately upon contact. It's not particularly durable so needs regular reapplication. It's only moderately water resistant and if it does get wet it water spots, looking like a late-stage leprosy. Today, specially formulated linseed oils for gunstocks, such as Lin-Speed and Brownell's Linseed

Oil, employ improved refining and added drying agents to solve the drying-time problem, but the others remain.

While boiled linseed oil was the standard of individual gunmakers and small shops, the mass production companies springing up in the latter half of the nineteenth century turned elsewhere. Varnish was coming into vogue and it alleviated many of the problems associated with the oil finish. Varnish doesn't penetrate into the wood to the degree of oil, but rather builds a hard, impervious coating on top of it. It dries fast, which is critical for mass production, and is not affected by heat and humidity. It also repels water much better than an oil finish as long as it remains intact. And therein lies the bugaboo of all built-up finishes, remaining intact. Once the skin is broken, moisture and air works its way under the finish, slowly loosening its grip on the wood. Early varnishes were quite brittle and over time were prone to crack, sometimes even forming a checkerboard of many cracks both vertically and horizontally. Also, some cleaning solvents dissolve varnish if left in contact too long. Nevertheless, most factory guns built from the late 1800's through the mid 1900's have some sort of varnish finish.

As I recall, Weatherby was one of first companies to pioneer the use of polymer finishes back in the 1950's. To keep this at ground level for us laypersons I'll just say polymer is a fancy term for plastic. In the case of wood finishes this usually means some form of epoxy or urethane. Gun afficianodos were used to the satiny glow of linseed oil and just slightly shinier varnish finishes. Polymer finishes shine like puddled water under stage lights. Some thought this new ultra shine was the next best thing to a voluptuous blonde while others, such as I, cringed at the gaudiness. However, love it or hate it, polymer was the wave of the future. It adheres better than regular varnish, is flexible so resists cracking, does not water spot, and is impervious to just about every chemical short of burning napalm. It is now used by most manufacturers. Like varnish, though, it is a built-up finish and if damaged it often gradually separates from the wood, leaving an ever enlarging bubble underneath.

One thing most polymers are not generally suited for is use by hobbyists. It is difficult to handle and apply and takes expensive spray equipment to come out with decent results. There is a vast array of other stock finishes designed for hobby and small shop use. There are the previously mentioned refined linseed oils. Tung oil, an oil derived from the seeds of the tropical tung tree, is similar to linseed oil but a bit shinier. My personal preference is for finishes that are a combination of oil and urethane

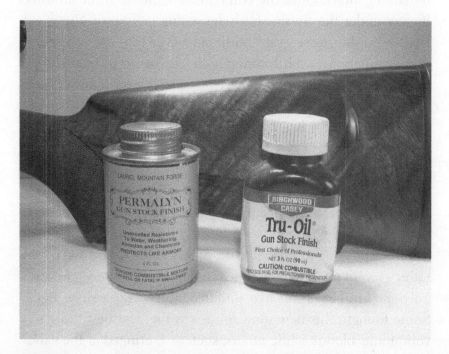

There are a number of stock finishes available for amateur use. Laurel Mountain Forge Permalyn is representative of the oil-modified urethanes which provide an oil-like finish vastly superior to linseed oil. Birchwood Casey Tru-Oil is a shiny finish resembling the plastic finish of most modern factory guns.

such as Permalyn Gunstock Finish and Pilkington Gunstock Finish. These pretty much provide the durability and chemical resistance of modern varnish with the ease of application and final look of an oil finish. There's also the old stand-by that's found in nearly every gun shop, Birchwood Casey Tru-Oil. Despite the name, it provides a very shiny, built-up varnish-type finish.

WOOD STOCK CARE & MAINTENANCE

The main goal of stock maintenance is to ensure the wood does not absorb undue amounts of moisture. Moisture may come from rain and snow, a dunking in a duck marsh, or, the most constant and pervasive, humidity in the air. Obviously, a good, water-resistant finish is important. It's easy to tell if the outer surfaces of a stock are sealed but what about those invisible areas? The inletting of the barrel, action, and bottom metal must be sealed or the stock will continually absorb and lose moisture with every humidity change. This is the most common cause of inconsistent performance, where the point of bullet impact changes from day to day or a gun shoots accurate one time and sprays bullets hither and yon the next. Swelling or shrinking around the action can put stress on critical areas and perhaps even cause the wood to split. If the wood underneath the buttplate and grip cap is not sealed the wood can swell here, too, causing unsightly fit.

Manufacturers are getting better at sealing these areas but let's start our maintenance program by checking. It's best to seal bare wood when the stock is in its driest stage. That means after the gun has been stored three to four weeks in a heated or air-conditioned room or during a natural period of low humidity. The best stuff for the job is wood sealer, available at any paint store. It penetrates the wood fairly well and quickly dries to a hard, watertight finish. It's not particularly durable but that's not a concern here. Brush it on, being careful to not get it on the external finish. Apply enough coats, letting each dry between applications, to saturate the wood completely. Don't allow copious build-up on the surface, though, or things may not fit so swell when you put her back together.

Stocks with varnish or modern polymer finishes in good condition need very little in the way of routine maintenance. Most of these finishes can be safely cleaned with alcohol, which doesn't leave any residue behind. Rarely will alcohol attack a varnish finish but try it on a small, inconspicuous spot first just to be sure. If the alcohol does soften the finish use soap and water (with all the metalwork removed from the stock, of course). Dish soap is a good choice because it's relatively mild yet cuts grease and oil well. Go easy on the water, just wiping it on and off, not hosing the whole works down. Avoid getting soap and water into the inletting. Be sure the stock is fully dried before reassembly.

Some people advocate regular applications of wax. Whether varnish or polymer, the finish is essentially a waterproof sheath much tougher than any wax, so nothing is accomplished in the way of protection. Wax does temporarily restore shine if that's to your liking. However, I advise against using wax because it can hinder future repair. Many waxes contain silicone and other petroleum distillates that are nigh-on to impossible to remove. In some cases they may even penetrate into the finish. This will affect the adhesion of additional finish applied during repairs. Even fully natural waxes such as carnuba are very difficult to remove completely from a finish.

As mentioned earlier, few, if any, production guns have an oil finish, that's more a product of custom shops and antiques. If you do have an oil-finished gunstock it will need regular attention. That is, of course, unless it's a valuable antique. These should not be mucked with. Being much less durable, oil tends to wear off during routine handling. Even sitting unused the finish will dry out over time. Depending on how much use the gun gets it should have another coat of oil once or twice a year. You can tell it's time when the finish loses its warm luster and takes on a dull look. This usually first occurs in the vicinity of the action where it is carried in the hand and on areas of end grain around the wrist and comb nose.

If replicating the original finish isn't important I'd suggest using an oil-modified urethane finish such as Permalyn or Pilkington Gunstock Finish, both available through Brownell's. These finishes are quantum leaps ahead of linseed or tung oil. They are more durable, more water resistant, don't water-spot, and are just as easy to apply as plain oil. The end result will, however, be shinier. Not gaudy shiny like varnish, but shinier than linseed oil. Since this is a care and maintenance book and not a gunsmithing guide, I will only detail adding maintenance coats to an existing finish. To finish a stock totally from scratch requires surface prep, pore filling, and other procedures that go beyond the scope of this mission.

Whether using oil or oil-modified urethane the procedure is the same. Remove everything from the stock—the metalwork, sling swivels, recoil pad, and such. Obviously, if the grip cap is permanently glued on it stays. The stock is probably all funky with hand sweat, deer blood, and dirt so clean it with alcohol. Let the stock stand fifteen minutes or so to allow all the alcohol to evaporate.

Touching the freshly oiled portion would leave fingerprints so now is the time to figure out how to hold on to the stock. We'll start applying oil at the butt, so we'll use the forend or front of the stock for a handle. It's that last little bit at the front that can be troublesome, sort of like painting yourself into a corner. If present, checkering provides a good gripping area with no worries of leaving fingerprints. Bolt rifles can be held by inserting your flattened hand into the magazine cut out. For stocks with a stock bolt hole, insert a tight fitting wooden dowel into the hole. Either taper an oversize dowel to fit or build up an undersized one with tape. Pistol grips can be held by the escutcheon screw inserted into its hole.

Freshly finished stocks have an uncanny penchant for falling over when just leaned against the wall so before oiling is also the time to formulate a way to hang the stock while it dries. Coat hangers can usually be bent and skeejawed in some fashion to attach to the stock without touching the newly oiled wood. A rod can be inserted into the action screw or stock bolt holes and clamped in the vise. It doesn't matter what you come up with, just devise it ahead of time, instead of when you have a handful of sticky gunstock.

With those potential problems solved, let's get on with it. Surely you've saved an old flannel or cotton-chamois shirt for just this occasion. Cut a square of flannel or similar tight-weave, absorbent cloth about five inches square. Brush out any lint or stray threads and wrap the cloth tightly over your first two fingers, holding it in place with your thumb. Dunk your cloth-covered fingertips into the oil, just lightly saturating the rag. Better too little oil than too much so err on the light side until you get a feel for it. The idea is to work the oil into the wood rather than flooding the wood surface.

Start working the oil into a small area of the buttstock with brisk, circular motions and a fair amount of pressure. When the area has absorbed all the finish it will, lightly wipe it off with a clean piece of flannel to ensure there's no standing oil on the surface then move on to the adjacent area. Oil-modified urethane turns tacky quite fast so keep the work area small. If it flips over on you before you get it off the surface simply wet it with fresh finish. At this stage it dissolves itself and can then be easily wiped off with the clean rag. Work on both sides of the stock equally as you progress forward. When oil begins to build up on the clean "wipe rag," switch to a new one. Liberally coat checkering with finger dunks of oil then immediately brush the oil back out of the grooves with a toothbrush. Brush out all you can, removing the excess oil with a rag.

With linseed oil, after the entire stock has been treated you're done. If using oil-modified urethane, however, you have an option. As previously mentioned, this tends to be shinier than linseed oil. The shine can be dulled some by continuing to buff the stock with a clean cotton rag until the finish sets. Every twenty minutes or so give the entire stock a light buffing. The shine will return soon after each buffing but eventually you will catch it at just the right time of finish set-up and the duller sheen

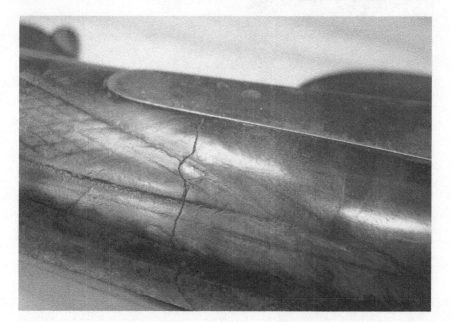

Small stock cracks are not always immediately obvious. Cleaning provides a good opportunity for close inspection.

will remain. This may happen quite soon or take up to a couple hours, depending on the temperature and humidity.

A trick of the trade to speed up drying of any finish, whether it be oil, varnish, polymer, or whatever, is to expose it to direct sunlight. I'm not sure what voodoo magic is involved, perhaps the ultraviolet rays, heat, or both, but it does wonders.

DAMAGE INSPECTION

Whenever we're fiddling with a gun under good light, as in cleaning, stock finishing, or whatever, keep a close eye out for stock damage. External damage is usually quite obvious. Dings in the finish easily catch our eye as would a large crack. Not always

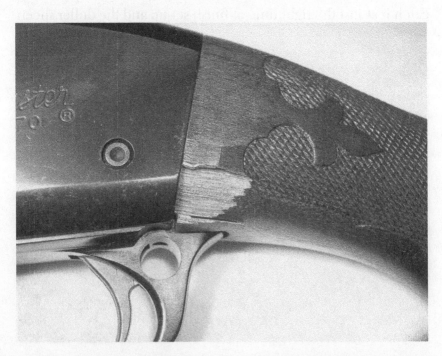

Two-piece stocks are especially prone to cracking and chipping where the buttstock mates with the receiver. This is caused by uneven inletting often enhanced by poor grain layout.

so obvious are smaller, hairline cracks. Cracks are most often caused by action metal continually pounding against the wood under recoil. The buttstock portion of two-piece stocks is notorious for cracking where the wood meets the action metal. If the inletting isn't in perfect, full contact with the action all the way around, the stock is likely to crack at some point in time.

Another equally bad offender is where a rounded portion of metal contacts the wood. This would be areas like at the rear of top and bottom action tangs and the rear of a sidelock action's lock plates. These rounded areas of metal act just like a wedge. While the unknowing consider gap-free inletting a sign of quality work, in these areas there should be a slight gap to avoid this.

The sidewalls of many pump and semi-auto shotgun forends are very thin and can easily crack for any number of reasons so keep a close eye on them. The toe of a buttstock is also prone to cracking because of the grain layout of the wood at this point. A sharp blow here, usually from the gun being dropped, can easily cause a crack or a piece actually to chip off.

Anytime a gun is disassembled we should inspect the stock for internal damage. Here again, the biggest culprit is cracks from metal banging against wood. Bolt actions that are improperly inletted or endure extreme recoil from Tyrannosaur Rex-slaying magnum cartridges can split behind the recoil lug. If the action fit is sloppy and the action screws bear against wood these can cause cracks at the screw holes. Internal cracks may also occur if the stock is incorrectly inletted and the action screws are really cranked down hard. Double barrel shotgun stocks, especially sidelocks, often have thin, delicate areas of wood in the action inletting that can crack or break off. Many traditional style muzzleloaders also have thin areas of wood around and underneath the lock that are prime places to crack.

WOOD STOCK REPAIR

While serious stock damage is best left to the professionals, most minor problems can be effectively dealt with by any hobbyist with moderate skills. The most common stock damage is a ding in the finish. Our concern here is exposed bare wood and, as previously discussed, air and moisture working underneath a varnish-type finish can cause the finish to lift away from the wood.

A first-class repair of a varnish or polymer finish is a delicate job. The biggest problem here is blending the repair into the surrounding finish. If it's just a minor surface scratch or blemish that doesn't expose wood I wouldn't worry about it. Simply buff the wound with a cloth and consider it a badge of experience. If it got down to the wood, though, it's time to go to work.

The polymer finish used on most factory guns is very durable but once the skin is broken through, moisture and air slowly loosen its grip on the wood causing a bubble to form under the finish. The loose finish must be completely removed before repair.

Clean the damaged area with alcohol, which won't raise the grain of the wood or cause discoloring. While doing so, note how well the color of the alcohol-wetted wood matches the rest. If it's close, you're lucky. If too light, it will have to be stained prior to finishing. The first step of repair is to remove all finish remnants within the damaged area as well as surrounding finish that is not firmly adhering to the wood. In some cases, especially with polymer finishes, there may even be a bubble under the finish at the damaged area. Use a hobby knife to gently pick and cut away any finish that easily lifts from the wood. Use some discretion here. Once clear of the damaged area, the finish should adhere strongly to the wood. In some cases, though, the original finish may not have stuck well to begin with. In that event you could peel the whole stock naked. Otherwise, just remove finish affected by the damage.

It's likely the wood is also damaged. Since we're not refinishing the whole stock, sanding out scratches and steaming out dents is not an option. Our best course is to use wood filler to fill dents and scratches to the original wood level. In days gone by, colored shellac sticks or a sawdust-glue paste were commonly used for this but I find the modern commercial wood fillers work much better and are infinitely easier to use. Wood filler is available at any paint or hardware store and comes in several colors. Pick a color slightly lighter than the wood under the surrounding finish. We can stain wood and filler darker but we can't make it lighter. Smoothing the dried filler usually requires some ingenuity, especially if the area is small. You can usually wrap wet-or-dry sandpaper around various shaped sticks and instruments to sand the filler without scratching the adjacent finish. A bent needle file works well, too. Again, the wood filler should be flush with the wood surface, not the finish.

With the wood repaired we're now left with a pockmark crater in the finish. Again wet the repair with alcohol (water will darken the wood too much) to see how close the color match is. The wood filler and perhaps the wood itself will probably need to be darkened. Staining to a perfect color match is an art that defies words. All I can say is give it your best shot, you'll probably get it close enough for government work. I like to use alcohol- or water-based wood dye but you seldom find these at your corner hardware store. My next choice is Min-Wax Wood Finish, which is readily available at paint stores. They call it a finish but it's really not. It's a thin, deep-penetrating stain that colors wood very well. Do not use stained varnish because we don't want a built-up finish yet. Allow the stain to dry completely, which in the case of Min-Wax takes several days.

With the damage repaired and color matched it's time to fill the crater left in the finish. For this we'll use clear, sandable wood sealer (with emphasis on sandable; some sealers are not designed to be sanded). Use a small artist's paintbrush to apply a heavy coat of sealer to the damaged area, being careful not to get sealer on the surrounding finish. Set aside to dry. As the sealer dries it shrinks considerably so it will take a number of coats to build the sealer up to the level of the finish. When the sealer is built up flush with the surface of the finish lightly sand the area with 1200-grit wet-or-dry sandpaper with a wood backer to blend it into the finish. Polish the sanded area using a clean felt polishing bob in a hand grinder. Do not use any polishing compound on the bob and run it at slow speed, always keeping it moving over the surface. If you hold the bob in one spot or run it too fast it will melt the finish. That's not good.

If the stock has a for real oil finish (which is rare) damage repair is easier. From a function perspective you could simply apply more oil to the damaged area. If you want to go to the effort, scratches and shallow dents can be sanded out prior to oiling. If the wood fibers have not been broken, more severe dents can be sanded to get below the original oil and then raised by dabbing hot water onto the dent. Stain as necessary with a penetrating stain and then work in the oil as described for recoating an oil-finished stock.

CRACK REPAIR

The repair of most stock cracks is also within the means of hobbyists. To deal with cracks we must have some general knowledge of glues and their use. Perhaps the most all-around useful and easiest to use is good-old carpenter's white wood glue. The key to success with this glue is the wood surfaces must be squeaky clean and perfectly mate to each other with no gap. If these criteria are met the bond will be stronger than the wood itself. The glue by itself, however, is brittle and easily breaks so it is not suitable for bridging even the slightest gap. It dries a translucent cream color and once dry cannot be stained.

When gaps or voids must be filled, epoxy is a good choice. I feel it also provides the strongest bond of all the common glues. We all know about epoxy, mix it precisely to instructions and work fast before it sets up. We also know it comes in regular and quick setting, or "five-minute" as it's often called. What you may not know is that the quick-set version only provides a little over half the bond strength of the regular. The quick-set is okay for powder-puff jobs but when the going gets tough reach for the real stuff. A particular nemesis of white carpenter glue is oil-soaked wood; it won't have any part of it. Epoxy will tolerate some oil, though the bond strength is severely diminished.

A relative newcomer on the woodworking scene is generically called super glue. The common super glues found down at the drug store generally don't work with wood and cannot fill cracks. There are some, however, such as Zap-A-Gap and Hot Stuff, that are designed for wood. Some versions are also capable

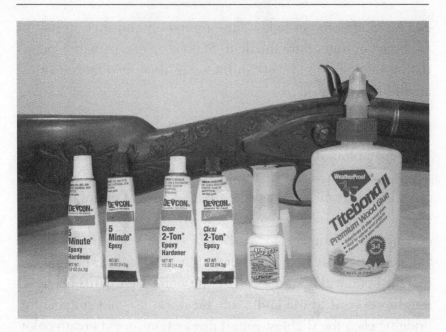

(Left to right): Epoxy is especially useful when a gap must be bridged. The quick-setting, 5-Minute version is fast but has much less strength than its longer-setting, 2-Ton brother. Super glues specially formulated for wood such as Zap-A-Gap wick into hairline cracks where other glues cannot go. Carpenter's white glue is easy to use and forms a bond stronger than the wood itself as long as the surfaces mate perfectly. It is not strong enough to fill gaps.

of filling minor gaps. The neat thing about super glues is they have little surface tension so they wick down into cracks like water. I haven't thoroughly tested this stuff for bond strength but from limited experience would rate it somewhat less than epoxy. It can also eat into some stock finishes or dry so fast it's hard to remove from unwanted places in time.

There are many other glue formulations on the market, each claiming to do one thing or another better than the others. This is probably fertile ground for experimentation but, quite frankly, I've yet to find a stock problem I couldn't solve with white glue, epoxy, or wood super glue. Okay, so much for Glue 101.

A crack doesn't just happen. Something caused it and we must figure out what so we can prevent it from reoccurring. Cracks behind tangs and sideplates are very common and are caused by the metal acting like a wedge when the gun recoils. Remove the metalwork from the stock. If the crack is tight with no gap we need to open it enough to get glue in. Working from inside the inletting where dings won't show, insert the tip of a hobby knife into the crack to try to spread it enough to accept glue. If that works, mix up a dab of real-deal epoxy, wedge the crack open, and use a thin-bladed tool or fine wire to work the glue as far down into the crack as you can. Remove the wedge, squeeze the wood to ensure it sets back in place and clean off the epoxy that oozed out. If you're artistic in your clean-up process, the epoxy may even serve as a finish over the crack.

If the crack can't be safely wedged open this is where the wood super glue finds its niche. Use the tip of a toothpick or straight pin to apply small amounts of super glue to the crack. Work fast to keep the glue wet and actively wicking in. Keep applying it until wicking stops. Immediately clean off excess glue.

Unfortunately, cracks are rarely that kind to us. More often they're a big, gaping canyon. With the metalwork removed, try to close the gap with a "C" clamp padded with pieces of thick leather. This may take some ingenious shimming because the surfaces are most always uneven or rounded. Don't overdue the clamp torque; it's only wood, you know. If the crack clamps neatly together, loosen the clamp, mix the epoxy and spread it evenly on both sides of the crack. Tighten the clamp, clean up the excess epoxy and call it a night. Let the epoxy completely cure before removing the clamp.

Now comes the worse scenario—the $#%&!$ crack just won't clamp together no matter what. There's no sense in putting the repair under stress so forget the clamp and deal with the crack as is. Work epoxy down into the crack but stop about one-thirty-second-inch short of entirely filling it up. Let the epoxy cure, then complete the repair with wood filler, and stain and finish with sealer as described in the finish-repair section.

Regardless of which technique was employed, the next step is to open up the inletting a smidgen to prevent the problem from reoccurring. Apply a thin coat of lipstick to the sides of the offending part and reassemble that portion of the gun. Remove the part and use a sharp hobby knife to scrape away areas of wood stained by the lipstick. This is patience time, removing just a little bit then recoating the part with lipstick and going through the process again . . . again . . . and again. The idea is to have the part fit into the wood with only a near microscopic gap between the wood and metal. At the rear of rounded parts such as action tangs the gap should be a bit more significant to allow for future set back.

A somewhat similar cause of cracks often occurs on guns with two piece stocks where the buttstock mates to the action. The wood here is quite thin and the constant pounding of recoil sometimes gets the better of it. In most cases the front of the stock is hollowed out to make room for the trigger assembly and other miscellaneous parts. That means we can get at the crack from the inside where our mucking around won't show. Experiment to find some means of clamping the crack together, perhaps with a leather padded "C" clamp, rubber bands, or tape. If worse comes to worst you may have to squeeze the crack together with your hands the forty-five minutes or so it takes the epoxy to set.

Epoxy is stronger than wood so if the crack is accessible from the backside we'll replace some of the wood with epoxy. Use a small, round router bit in a hand grinder to cut a channel along the length of the crack. This should be about two-thirds the depth of the wood and centered directly over the crack. Mix up an appropriate amount of full-strength epoxy to fill this channel. First work epoxy into the crack, wedging the crack open with a tool if necessary. Once the crack is well coated, fill the routed channel full of epoxy. Clamp the crack together, clean excess glue from the outer stock surface and set aside to cure in such a manner that the glue won't run out of the channel.

After the epoxy has fully cured we'll check the inletting where the front of the stock mates to the action. The stock must be in full contact with the metal all the way around to lessen chances of future splitting. Apply a thin, even coat of lipstick to the back of the action metal and install the stock. Remove the stock and note where lipstick has been transferred to the wood. If the stock does not show lipstick all the way around, scrape away the lipstick stained areas, which are the high spots, with a hobby knife. I find the rounded knife blade the best for this. If it's obvious you have a long ways to go use a fine toothed triangular file

Internal cracks such as this one behind the recoil lug can be easily repaired by grinding out the crack, stopping just short of the stock surface, and filling the trench with long setting epoxy or stock-bedding compound. If the gun is a hard kicker, installing a cross bolt prior to the epoxy would be good insurance.

for the bulk of the hogging and finish up by scraping. Repeat this procedure, recoating the action with lipstick each time, until full wood-to-metal contact is attained.

Often, rather than these buttstocks just cracking, a piece breaks all the way off. If you have the piece it can be replaced using the same techniques as crack repair. If the piece is long gone a new one can be made and attached. Obviously, this entails not only making the piece, but fitting the joint and staining and finishing to match the rest of the stock. If you have the skills for this you don't need further input from me. Otherwise, it's best to just take it to a pro.

SYNTHETIC STOCK MAINTENANCE AND REPAIR

Today's synthetic stocks are made from a variety of materials, the most common being fiberglass, Kevlar, graphite, boron, and combinations thereof. Fiberglass has been around since dirt and was the original synthetic stock material. It's still the best for all around strength and damage resistance. It is on the heavy side, though. When Kevlar came along it was considered the wonder material of the century. It's some lighter than fiberglass and, when set in resin, more rigid. It's the material used in bullet-proof vests and firemen's protective clothing. It's not very abrasion resistant but that's a moot point for gunstocks as it's protected by an overcoat of resin. Graphite's claim to fame is it is very lightweight. Unfortunately, it's quite brittle and breaks relatively easily. To lessen this problem it's often used in conjunction with boron, Kevlar, or fiberglass.

These materials are woven into cloth, saturated with epoxy type resin, and molded to form a thin outer skin in the shape of a stock. This skin usually averages about an eighth-inch thick, give or take a little. The inner core is most always some type of lightweight, foam-like material. This dual construction is necessary to keep the weight at an acceptable level.

One reason for the popularity of synthetic stocks is that they require very little maintenance. About the only maintenance worth doing is to wash the crud off now and then. A rag and dish soap will suffice for this. The hard, tough, outer shell is impervious to chemicals and won't easily dent, scratch, or crack. Should a minor scuff or scratch occur it can be touched up with paint. Most unpainted synthetic stocks are a dull-black color which can be closely matched with matte-black enamel. This is commonly available at most paint stores. Apply it with a small artist's brush.

Often synthetic stocks are painted in some camouflage pattern or sometimes with wrinkle-finish paint to improve grip. Of course, this paint is susceptible to damage and wear. A few scratches here and there don't hurt a thing, just consider it additional camouflage. If a large area is worn off, though, you may want to refurbish it. Camo spray paint in a variety of colors is available through Brownell's. Some sporting-goods and paint stores carry them as well. These paints are usually enamel which requires a primer base coat for best results. There are other hi-tech camo paints that may or may not take primer. Go by the label.

Clean the area to be repainted with alcohol. If called for, spray on a thin base coat of primer and allow it to dry fully. Most camo patterns are realistic images of vegetation. If artistic talent wasn't in your gene pool you can just randomly squirt some various colored blobs and stripes and call it better than it once was. I guarantee the critter you're fixin' to shoot won't notice the discrepancy. However, if Rembrandt is surging through your veins use artist's brushes to apply the paint, duplicating the original pattern to the best of your abilities. Camo paint usually comes in spray cans so just squirt some into the can's cover to dip out of. You can lay out some basic pattern guide lines with a very soft lead pencil but the graphite will affect the paint adhesion so erase them ahead of you as you go.

Applying wrinkle-finish paint is a no-brainer. This, too, is available through Brownell's as well as some automotive stores. Simply clean the area to be painted with alcohol, prime if necessary, and apply a couple of heavy coats according to instructions.

Whenever you remove a synthetic stock from the action keep a sharp eye out for powdery dust. If this appears each time the stock is removed it may mean the lightweight core material of the stock is degrading or there's something significantly wrong with the inletting. Have it checked by a gunsmith knowledgeable in synthetic stocks.

Minor adjustments to synthetic stock dimensions such as raising the comb or changing the grip shape can be made with automotive body filler. This can be found at any automotive store. Lightly sand the area to receive the filler with 100-grit sandpaper to remove paint and scuff the surface so the filler gets a good grip. Remember, that shell isn't very thick so go easy. Mix an appropriate amount of filler and apply it where needed as smooth and evenly as possible. There's a short period of time, five to ten minutes, after the filler sets up but before it gets serious about curing. That's when the filler can be easily carved with a sharp chisel. Do crude smoothing and shaping then. When fully cured, finish shaping with rasp and sandpaper and prime and paint to match the stock finish. Unless it's a target rifle or varminter where weight isn't an issue I advise against major shape changes. Large amounts of filler will noticeably affect stock weight and overall balance.

Chapter 12

SCOPES, SCOPE MOUNTS, AND OPEN SIGHTS

SIGHTING IN A SCOPE

This may be stretching the care and maintenance theme a bit but in my mind a gun isn't properly cared for unless it's sighted in and ready to go. Many shooters have great difficulties sighting in a gun. You see it almost daily at the range. A neophyte with a newly mounted scope shows up, hangs a target at the one-hundred-yard bunker, rests his elbows on the bench, and starts blazing away. The shots are missing the target in a variety of unknown directions so he starts randomly spinning the adjustment dials, hoping by some miracle a bullet will somehow hit the paper to give him a point to work from. When his box of ammo is fruitlessly expended he stomps off in frustration.

Obviously, a gun is only as accurate as the person shooting it. You have to do your part. This is no place to be showing off your shooting skills or lack thereof. Take as much human error out as possible by using a rock solid bench and good sandbags. Nothing works like sand. Certain techniques must be followed to shoot effectively from a bench rest. Stack several bags for the forend to rest on and place another, smaller bag under the toe of the buttstock. The front bags should be positioned just slightly forward of the action, not way out on the forend.

With the gun just lightly shouldered, shift and squeeze the front bags around until the crosshairs are aligned just slightly above the bullseye. Take a very light grip with your trigger hand and use your off hand to squeeze the rear bag, raising the butt of the gun to bring the crosshairs into perfect alignment. Reach around the front bags and lightly grasp the forend. Be sure the gun is resting naturally on the bags and you are not steering it with shoulder, cheek or either hand. You should be able to let go of the gun and back away without it moving even the slightest. Take three or four deep breaths, letting the last one out only half way. Gently sque-e-e-e-ze the trigger. When the gun goes off it should startle you right out of your shorts. For eye-crossing, shoulder-tenderizing T. Rex slayers hold the gun firmly to your shoulder and hang on tighter with both hands but still take care not to steer the gun in any way.

The first step in sighting in a scope is to get the crosshairs aligned well enough for the shot at least to hit the target. A scope collimator does this easily but they are expensive and few casual shooters can justify the luxury. Forget that hundred-yard bull (pun intended). Reduce the margin of error by setting up at twenty-five yards. If the gun is a bolt action which allows us to re-move the bolt and see through the bore we can first bore sight it before burning up ammo. Shore the gun up steady on a bench with sandbags. Peer down through the bore and adjust the gun so the target is centered in the bore. Without moving the gun, ad-just the scope so the crosshairs are also centered on the target. The first shot at this distance should be reasonably close.

If the action type does not lend itself to bore sighting you'll just have to hope for the best. Attach a target to a large piece of cardboard at the twenty-five yard line. Shoot from the bench with sandbags. With luck, the first shot at least hits the cardboard, if not the target. If not, you should be able to see in what direction it missed. Adjust the scope accordingly. Virtually all scopes have markings on the adjustment dials for a guide. Most also click at each adjustment mark. Each mark or click is supposed to move the bullet impact point some precise distance at one hundred yards. I say "supposed to" because some inexpensive brands (and even some high-dollar models) don't always do as promised. Depending on the scope, one click may be the equivalent of one-quarter, one-half or even one inch at one hundred yards. At twenty-five yards you have to adjust the scope four times as many clicks to move a given distance as you do at one hundred yards. If you don't know where the shot went move the target closer. Once there's a bullet hole on the paper you have it made. Align the crosshairs on the bullet hole with the rifle firmly supported by sandbags. Taking great care to not move the gun (a helper is handy, here), adjust the crosshairs so they are centered on the bull's-eye. The next shot should be dead center at this distance.

In theory, you should now be able to move the target to one hundred yards and only have to make a slight adjustment to compensate for the change in the bullet flight path. In reality, you'll probably save ammo in the long run by re-zeroing at fifty yards, then moving to one hundred yards for final tuning. At fifty yards you'll have to use twice as many clicks as you would at one hundred yards. From fifty yards and beyond never trust just one shot for making adjustments. If two consecutive shots are very close together go ahead and adjust. Otherwise, shoot three or even five and use the center of the group as the reference point. If the scope is a variable, at these longer distances set it at the highest power setting for maximum accuracy. Scopes are not supposed to change their zero while going back and forth in magnification but, again, you can't count on it. Once dialed in at high magnification, drop back to the power you use most often and try a few shots there to be sure.

SCOPE MAINTENANCE

Virtually all modern scopes are made of aluminum with an anodized finish. They don't rust and the finish is tough so routine maintenance requirements are very minimal. Dust and debris can be simply wiped off the scope body. The scope body does not need to be protected with rust preventive unless the anodized finish is damaged or worn through. In this case, rust preventive will help guard against corrosion until the damage can be repaired,

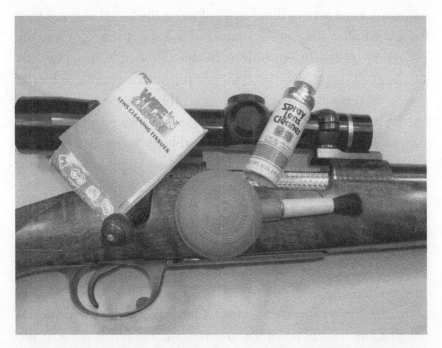

Precision lenses with delicate coatings is where all the big money for scopes goes. Don't trash out those lenses with a shirttail or rag. First, gently remove loose particles that could scratch the lens with a bulb air brush. Follow up with a quality lens cleaner and lens cloths.

which we will soon get to. Depending on the brand, scope rings and mounts may be blued steel that should have a coat of rust preventive.

Lenses occasionally need cleaning and this is one task not to be taken lightly. This is where all of those big bucks you laid out for the scope went and they can be very easily damaged. The lenses are coated with some kind of magical stuff to bring out the best optical qualities and we must take care not to scratch or abrade this coating. Start by removing all the dust and debris that has a way of taking up residence on the lenses. This is best done with those combination squeeze air bulb and soft brush tools used to clean camera lenses. First blow away all the debris you can with the air, then use the brush to loosen anything stuck to the lens, blowing it away with the bulb, too. Lacking the air bulb, simply blow the dust away with your breath and use a cotton-tipped swab to gently remove stuck particles.

To remove water spots, air-borne grease, and such from the lenses use camera or eyeglass lens cleaning solution and several lens-cleaning cloths. You've heard it a hundred times but I'll make it one hundred and one, never use a hanky or rag. One little grain of grit or even the coarse weave of the cloth can damage the lens coating. A clean, cotton-tipped swab can be used to get into the corners. Remove the cleaning solution before it evaporates as it may leave a film on the lens. Forget any temptations to use things like windshield anti-fogging chemicals and such on the lenses. They could damage the coating or, at the very least, leave a film that hinders the optical quality.

Every now and then check the scope adjustment caps to be sure they are tight. Some caps employ rubber seals which can deteriorate or go missing. If they need replacing, you'll probably have to order them from the manufacturer so get a spare set while you're at it.

If the anodized finish on the scope body is damaged or worn exposing bare aluminum a bit of paint will hide the defect and keep the aluminum from corroding. A paint designed for aluminum like Brownell's Aluma-Hyde II is best. Most paints require a special aluminum primer be applied first but not this one. It's also resistant to high-powered bore solvents that eat up standard paints in a heartbeat. Aluminum begins corroding the moment it is exposed to air so it must be cleaned and the corrosion removed just moments prior to painting. For small areas use an artist's paintbrush. If the area is more extensive you may choose to spray it right from the aerosol can. Follow the preparation and application instructions on the label.

SCOPE MOUNTING SYSTEMS

Few shooters put much thought into scope mounts but they deserve as much consideration as the scope itself. Obviously, they must be strong, which isn't much of an issue in this day and age. Any company making wimpy mounts isn't in business long. Whether aluminum or steel, all the name-brand mounts fill this bill. I place great importance in mounting the scope as low as possible. Most factory gun stocks are dimensioned for use with open sights. The higher the scope the more you'll have to rubberneck your head up off the stock to see through it. Not only is that awkward, if your cheek isn't firmly planted on the comb the stock jumps up under recoil and whacks you in the mug. The next thing you know you're flinching with each shot like a horse astraddle an electric fence.

Another thing I'm very fond of is quick-detachable scope mounts. These mounts allow the scope to be removed quickly with the flip of two levers. Scopes are great when all is well, but . . . Like the time I was rowing the shore of a lake during one of northern Canada's infamous, never-ending drizzles. A very

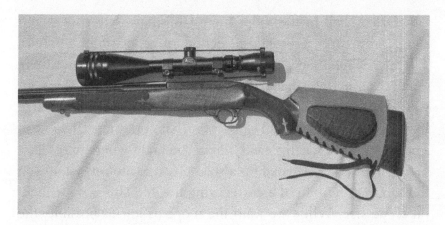

With large scopes such as this one on the author's tricked-out Ruger 10/22 or for unusually high scope mounts the stock comb must be raised to provide the proper sight picture. Though not the prettiest arrangement, a lace-on leather riser is an inexpensive alternative to restocking.

respectable bull moose stepped out of the bushes about eighty yards away. As rifle came to shoulder all I could make out through the scope was a blurry, black blob. The lenses were covered with half frozen water. My hankie was buried deep under rain gear and vigorously shaking the rifle was no help. No worries. I flipped the detachable scope levers, took a bead with the open sights and laid him to rest. Then there was the wounded Cape buffalo that made his last stand in brush so thick the scope was nothing but a liability. A scope aimed towards a low sun completely whites out. All is not always well with scopes and with a serious hunting gun I want immediate access to the open sights.

Yes, I'm aware of see-through mounts which allow you to see the open sights through an opening below the scope. However, as previously mentioned, that raises the scope so high I find myself bobbing and weaving my head around to find the sight picture. Quick-detachable mounts are frightfully expensive, though, so I use traditional mounts on guns for more casual duty such as varminters, small-game and target guns, and fun plinkers.

Okay, back to the scope-mount business. Most local gun shops only carry a limited selection of scope-mount brands. There are literally dozens of different styles available and there may be something that better suits your needs than what's on your dealer's shelf. Perusing the Internet and catalogs of large mail-order firms is a good way to see what's out there. If you can find your choice locally, great, if not, you know where to get it.

Once you've decided on a style of scope-mount system you then must determine the correct ring height. This is dependent on scope size. While we want the scope as low as possible, the rings must be high enough for the front objective lens housing to clear the barrel and, on bolt action rifles, for the bolt handle to clear the rear of the scope. If it's an old military rifle the swing safety on the rear of the bolt can also be an issue.

Unfortunately, there's no universal standard for measuring ring height. Most manufacturers use the nomenclature low, medium, and high with a few adding ultra-low and extra high. The actual measurements of these designations vary from manufacturer to manufacturer. Some makers measure from the base of the ring to the center of the ring where the scope reticles would cross. Others measure from the base of the ring to the bottom inside of the ring where it contacts the scope body.

The best way to determine ring height is to take your gun and scope to a gun shop carrying a large selection of mounting systems and just try them. Similarly, you can mail-order low, medium, and high rings, select the best and return the others. If you have a set of rings of the style you want on another rifle you can use these as a gauge. Try them with the new scope and gun to determine if that height is okay or if they need to be higher or lower. Many catalogs list the actual ring-height measurement which can be used for reference. If none of those methods work for you, attach the base to the rifle and make a square wooden block to go between base and scope that holds the scope at just the right height. Measure the block and choose a ring height that comes closest to that.

Before discussing the installation of the scope I am compelled to digress. Do you have any idea where your gun shoots with the open sights? I learned the hard way that open sights can save the day. On another fly-in moose hunt prior to the one just described I was in such a remote part of Canada even the black flies had a hard time finding me. Climbing an immense boulder at river's edge I slipped, bounced, and banged down the face of the rock and belly flopped into the deep river. I managed to hang on to the rifle throughout these antics but upon hauling myself out I found the scope filled with water. Though the water easily made its way in, nary a drop would come back out. The rifle was a minimally sporterized Springfield '03 with no open sights. I was the official camp tender for the rest of the trip. Yes, open sights are that important. Before mounting the scope why not go to the range and sight in those open sights?

INSTALLING MOUNTS AND SCOPES

The hardest part of this whole scope-mounting business is finding the right ring height. Once past that, the installation is a piece of cake, assuming the gun is already drilled and tapped, of course. If not, a trip to the gunsmith is in order for that is not a job for rookies. Even though we're dead-bang certain all our calculations were right it's still prudent to do a trial installation before cinching everything down. Screw the base onto the action, just lightly snugging the screws down. Install the rings on the scope leaving them free to move back and forth. Properly align the rings to the base then attach them to the base. If the system is like Redfield or Leupold, where a lug on the bottom of the front ring locks into the base by turning the scope, attach the rings to a wooden dowel rather than the scope and use the dowel to turn the lug in this first time. This precludes any chance of bending the scope if the lug fit is particularly tight. Put some grease on the lug, too. Once the rings are seated remove the dowel and mount the scope.

Now shoulder the rifle from various shooting positions to ensure there's enough back-and-forth scope adjustment for proper eye relief. The rings should not bear directly against the lens housings or the adjustment turret in the middle. If eye relief is not right we'll have to go to plan B. Some two-piece bases can be turned around in the front, back, or both to change the ring position. Some manufacturers also offer extension bases that reposition the rings. If neither of these are an option you'll have to switch mounting-system brands.

Once the scope is positioned for proper eye relief, lightly snug the ring screws down and work the bolt, safety, and anything else the scope may interfere with. If problems are encountered you'll either have to go to higher rings or modify the part. For instance, sometimes the bolt handle can be bent or ground down or a military safety can be replaced with a side swing safety to alleviate problems.

Another common problem is the base screws extending too far through the action and binding the bolt or other working parts. Note how much the screws need to be shortened and grind or file them to proper length. A small hand grinder with an abrasive wheel or sanding drum makes short work of this task. After shortening, taper the last little bit of thread at the screw tip with a knife-edge needle file to allow the screw to start in the threads. When you're sure everything is hunky-dory, place a piece of tape on the scope next to a ring to mark the proper scope location and dissemble everything.

Now it's time for semi-permanent installation (assuming the open sights are properly sighted in). A lot of hassles come from scope-mount screws working loose from repeated recoil. To remove that from our worry list we'll use Loc-Tite Thread-Locker in several different strengths. This can be found in almost any hardware and automotive stores. Thoroughly clean all the base and ring screws and their corresponding threaded holes with evaporating solvent or lacquer thinner. Use a toothbrush to clean the screws and a cotton-tipped swab for the holes. Pull enough cotton off the swab to allow it to be turned into the holes. Saturate a small piece of cloth with rust preventive and carefully apply a thin coat to all the metal surfaces of the base, rings, base and ring screw heads and top of the action. Be sure no rust preventive gets on any of the threads.

Applying Loc-Tite to screws ensures they won't work loose. Medium strength No. 242 (blue) allows most screws to be removed without special measures and is the one most suitable for general firearm use. High strength No. 271 (red) requires heating the parts with a torch to remove the screw so is used only in the most dire circumstances. Not shown, low strength No. 222 (purple) may be preferable for small screws that are often removed.

For the base screws we'll use medium strength Loc-Tite No. 242 (blue). This version of Loc-Tite effectively secures screws yet they can still be removed without taking drastic measures (as in heating with a torch, which is required with full strength, red Loc-Tite No. 271). Apply the blue Loc-Tite to the base screws and their corresponding holes (one at a time) and install the base. Immediately clean up the excess Loc-Tite that oozes out, including inside the action.

If you think you'll be removing the scope from time to time, perhaps to switch it to another gun or whatever, consider using low strength No. 222 Loc-Tite (purple) for the ring screws. However, if you're headed off on that hunt of a lifetime I'd go with the blue No. 242 for added insurance. Before securing the ring screws, though, we must ensure the scope's crosshairs are perfectly level.

Clamp the rifle in a padded jaw vise and aimed at a distant wall. Lacking that, rest it securely on sandbags. Either way, be sure the gun is straight up and down with no sideways canting. Hang a string with an attached weight to the wall and align the vertical crosshair to this. While tightening the ring screws, uneven torque may turn the scope slightly, rotating the crosshairs off level. It helps to tighten the screws gradually, switching from side to side and front ring to back ring as you go. Since this may take some fiddling and a retry or two, install the scope without Loc-Tite on the ring screws, then go back and apply it to one screw at a time while leaving the others firmly cinched down. A common error when installing scope ring screws is not getting them tight enough, especially on the big kickers. A few shots later the scope has crept forward and messed up the eye relief. Only experience can tell you the difference between a really tight screw and a stripped thread or broken one, but they'll withstand more reefing than you may think.

Many popular scope-mount systems such as Weaver, Redfield, and Leupold in one way or another secure one or both rings to the base with large screw heads. These usually serve more or less as quick-detach mounts, sideways scope adjustments, or both so I generally don't apply Loc-Tite to these.

OPEN SIGHTS

Open sights are the height of simplicity and seldom require much attention other than ensuring they are correctly sighted in. With most adjustable open sights the adjustments are made with the rear sight. *Move the rear sight in the same direction you want the bullet to move on the target.* How far to move it is generally determined by trial and error. If the maximum elevation adjustment of the rear sight doesn't get you far enough, further adjustment can be had by installing a higher or lower front sight. There are a host of aftermarket sights of varying heights available. Adjustment with the front sight is determined *in the opposite direction you want the bullet impact to move on the target.*

In some cases the rear sight is moved up and down for elevation changes and the front sight must be moved for windage corrections. Front sights are usually attached by dovetail with friction holding them in place. Use a brass punch and hammer to drift the sight from side to side. Again, when adjusting the front sight, it is moved in the opposite direction you want the bullet to move on the target.

Non-adjustable sights can sometimes be altered to make elevation changes. If the front sight is the blade type it can be filed down to raise bullet impact. To lower bullet impact file the rear-sight notch deeper.

OPEN-SIGHT REPAIR

For the most part, open sights are pretty trouble free. The most common malady is damage or loss of the front bead. These are usually attached by dovetail and a replacement, either from the manufacturer or an aftermarket source, can be easily installed. When dealing with dovetails the rule of protocol is to drive the part in from right to left when looking from the rear of the gun. With the gun lying flat on the bench, support the sight ramp with an appropriately sized hardwood block to minimize stress to it. Do the bulk of the driving with a nylon hammer and finish up setting it flush in the slot, or beyond if necessary, with a brass punch.

If the sight is too tight in the dovetail and absolutely refuses to go in, don't try to take metal off the angled sides as would seem logical. Carefully remove a small amount of metal from the bottom of the sight with a fine-toothed flat file, which accomplishes the same thing only better and easier. The final fit must be very tight so only remove a tiny bit of metal at a time and take care to keep the bottom of the sight perfectly flat and true. If it's too loose to stay put use a pointed punch and hammer to raise a few dimples on the bottom. Stone them to the right height by trial and error fitting.

Shotgun beads commonly break off or work loose and disappear. Replacement beads of all styles and sizes are available from Brownell's. Check the thread size by finding a screw that properly threads into the hole and then measure the screw threads. If the bead is broken off, leaving the stump in the hole, remove it with an E-Z Out as described in screw repair in the troubleshooting chapter. If it's fighting you zealously heat the barrel a bit with a propane torch but go easy lest you cook the bluing. Bluing can usually withstand up to about 400 degrees or a trifle more but you don't want to get anywhere near that. Clean the screw and barrel threads with evaporating degreaser and anchor the bead in once and for all with slow-cure epoxy. If it extends down into the barrel, *very carefully* grind it flush with a hand grinder at slow speed. I find the cone-shaped grinding bobs the easiest to control for this delicate job.

The brass sight beads commonly found on both rifles and shotguns tarnish and become dull over time. Brighten them up with No. 0000 steel wool. Some folks prefer a white-colored bead. This can be easily achieved with white paint and a fine artist's brush. To preserve its brightness longer apply a clear top coat that is compatible with the paint used. Your local paint store can tell you what works with what.

Another common problem occurs with rear sights that adjust by sliding up and down on a dovetailed ramp. Tiny screws are supposed to keep them securely in place. Especially on hard kickers, these sights may refuse to stay put under recoil. Often this problem stems from not being able to tighten the screw properly because you don't have the right-sized screwdriver. If

Sights such as this Truglo incorporating light-gathering, fiber-optic rods are inexpensive and a blessing for old, tired eyes. They are available both front and rear in a variety of configurations and heights.

necessary, shape a screwdriver to fit the slot perfectly so you can cinch the screw down good and tight. If that fails, note the proper position for the sight, apply a coat of flexible glue — such as Barge cement — to it and then tighten the screw. The glue won't permanently set the sight in yet may provide enough extra grip to hold it in place. If the threads of the screw become stripped you can try restoring them with Loc-Tite Thread Restorer or similar product but it will likely require sight replacement.

There's a disturbing phenomenon going on with gun sights. Recently I've discovered that sights know when old, tired eyes such as mine are looking through them and they instantly turn dark and grow a coat of fuzz. To combat this there are a variety of aftermarket sights utilizing light-gathering, fiber-optic rods both as a front bead and to outline the rear notch. William's Fire Sight and Truglo are common examples for rifles and handguns and Hi Viz has long been on the market for shotguns. There are many other brands as well. The only downside I've found is the plastic rods are a bit fragile but Brownell's carries replacement rods in a variety of sizes for a quick, easy fix. Along these lines are lithium and tritium sights that actually glow in the dark. These are knee-buckling expensive and, quite frankly, I don't see the purpose for sporting use. Most countries outlawed night hunting long ago.

Chapter 13

ACCOUTREMENTS

SLINGS

All will agree that a good sling is imperative on a hunting gun. What makes a good sling is largely a matter of personal preference, I suppose, but I'll throw out some food for thought. One thing I don't like is a wide sling. The additional weight distribution feels good while standing in the store but when out brush busting and scaling mountains a wide sling continually slips down my shoulder. It also seems more cumbersome, stiff, and in the way when taking a hasty rest over a tree limb or rock. The old, standard one-inch leather sling is the most amenable to me. It digs into my shoulder just enough to stay put and when well oiled the leather is just the right stiffness.

While I have a penchant for leather slings, especially on fine, high grade guns, a case can certainly be made for nylon. It doesn't require any care, quickly dries after getting wet, never rots or cracks and is as strong as a tow-truck cable. The nylon surface is slippery, though, and slides around on your shoulder like a greased snake. I strongly suggest getting one with the shoulder area lined with leather or, better yet, some form of rubber to prevent this. If you don't mind a plastic strap on your gun, go for it; it's certainly practical.

Some slings are designed to form an adjustable loop at the front to wrap around your forearm while shooting. This is commonly taught in the military and if you know how to do right it helps to steady your aim while shooting off hand. Having washed out of the Army with a bum back I never practiced this style of shooting enough to be comfortable with it. Give me a tree limb or rock rest any day. Such a sling is worth consideration, though.

While nylon slings are maintenance free, not so with leather. Leather slings need treating every now and then to keep them from drying out and cracking. Usually, once or twice a year will suffice. What to use for this depends on how the leather was tanned. With most tanning processes the leather is best treated with Neatsfoot Oil, available at shoe stores. Apply it in finger

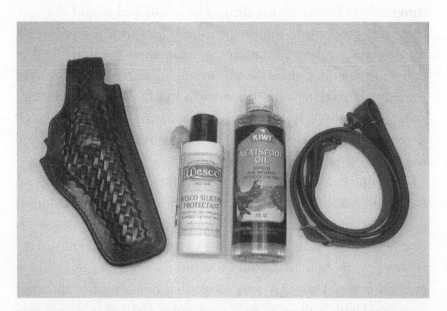

All leather items from slings and holsters to gun cases need regular applications of leather conditioner to keep them from drying out and cracking. What to use depends on how the leather was tanned. Most firearm accoutrements are best treated with Neatsfoot Oil. Some, however, may require silicone (both are available at shoe stores). Check the product manual or consult the manufacturer.

dunks and work it in until the leather is totally saturated then wipe off any excess standing on the surface. I don't recommend boot grease as it leaves a tacky coating on the surface that collects dirt and stains your clothing. Leather specially tanned to be waterproof usually requires treating with liquid silicone, also available at shoe stores. If the packaging doesn't include treating instructions ask the manufacturer, for using something not compatible with the tanning process can screw up the leather.

SLING SWIVELS

Sling-swivel systems come in a variety of styles from simple, non-detachable ones to custom works of art. The swivel base either screws into the stock or is attached to the stock with screws. A loop to hold the sling then attaches to the base either permanently or in a quickly removable fashion. All serve the purpose but the quick-detachable type is much handier. Some folks worry about the detaching system being weak or failing but I've used them exclusively for over forty years without a single problem.

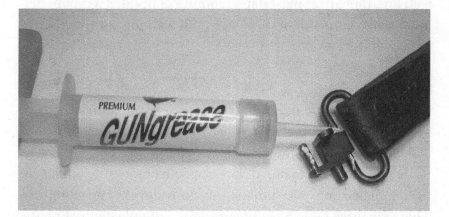

Sling swivels should be regularly lubricated to keep them from squeaking and prevent rust. The author prefers grease for this job, assuming it can be worked in between parts. If not, oil.

Sling swivels are made of steel so take the same rust preventing precautions as with the rest of the gun. In addition, apply grease to the moving parts of the swivel to prevent squeaking.

HANDGUN HOLSTERS

Much of the dissertation on slings applies to holsters as well. They are typically made of leather or nylon. Leather holsters have the advantage of being formed to provide a perfect fit for a particular model of gun, something that can't be done well with nylon. I'm not sure how important that is in the sporting arena, though. Of course, nylon is virtually maintenance free. Style is entirely up to you and your needs. I prefer shoulder holsters mostly because I have this image thing against folks strutting around like John Wayne with a big shootin' iron hanging down their leg. In my mind it doesn't portray a sense of responsibility. In a shoulder holster even a big buffalo-stomping gun can be concealed from view and protected from brush and the elements under a jacket. It also doesn't interfere with fairly important things like walking and sitting down. Check out the legal issues with this, though, as most states require a concealed weapons permit to carry a gun out of view. Heed this warning because law enforcement gets serious about this.

GUN CASES

Cases are one of the most important items in our array of firearm accessories. After all, they're what stand between our firearms and harms way. They must not be used for storage because even if made of breathable material they can collect moisture and cause rusting. Their job is to protect our guns during transportation. There are three basic types of gun cases, a simple cloth or plastic sleeve, the padded soft case, and the hard case. The sleeve type is of marginal use. Being just a single layer of material it affords no

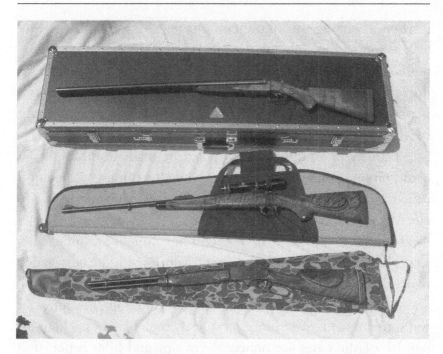

Guns must never be stored in cases; they're solely for protection while traveling. (Top to bottom): A quality hard case of aluminum or heavy plastic is imperative for airline and long-distance or rough-vehicle travel. A padded soft case is perfect for day-to-day transportation where the hard case would be too cumbersome. The simple cloth sleeve provides almost no protection and is next to useless.

damage protection. It satisfies the law in states that require guns to be cased during transportation and if made of plastic it would provide a barrier to the elements but that's about it.

Padded soft cases, on the other hand, are a gun-owner's best friend. The padding affords protection against abrasion and minor blows and when not in use it can be folded up and stored without taking up too much space. For general use it should be made of soft, breathable cloth or leather. Those made of plastic are notorious for trapping in moisture and causing rusting. The only time I would consider using a plastic case is when protection from the elements was a major factor. Even then I would only use it when a soaking was imminent and remove the gun from the case as soon as possible. I like padded soft cases that are very flexible so they can be easily folded up and tucked in a pack. It seems the recent trend is for stiff ones. To me these are a bit of a bastard, neither soft nor hard. I'm not asking it to do the job of a hard case so what's the point?

Hard cases for utilitarian purposes are made from stiff plastic or aluminum. These come into play when the utmost protection is called for, as in airline baggage, for shipping, or long trips in a vehicle. Aluminum cases are by far the strongest but are heavier than a dead moose and expensive. The cost and weight are more than worth it, though, when the going gets really tough. The best quality hard plastic cases can also withstand all but the most extreme abuse. Just be sure the construction is good and stout, meaning stiff walls, metal piano-style hinge, and beefy metal latches. The inexpensive plastic cases are noticeably wimpy and little better, if as good, as a soft padded case. Of course, hard cases are cumbersome and best reserved for distance traveling. Once at the final destination I switch to a soft padded case for day to day use.

There are other case styles such as leather or canvas-covered wood and the old "leg-o'-mutton" cases made of very thick, stiff leather but these are mostly a matter of elitism and more for show than go.

Just about every gun nut has a closet full of gun cases but it's really not necessary. It's far better to go for quality than quantity. If you had three soft padded cases, one for scoped rifles, a narrower one for shotguns, and one for handguns and two hard cases, one sized for all your long guns and another for handguns, you'd be good to go anywhere and do anything. Of course, if your pursuits involve transporting multiple guns at once your inventory would need to be upped accordingly. Hard cases that hold two guns are also available. Personally, I don't care for them.

They are by necessity huge and heavy, especially the aluminum ones, and it takes an entourage of gun bearers to lug the things around. If they tickle your fancy, though, don't let me talk you out of them.

Gun cases don't require much in the way of maintenance. I can't emphasize enough not to use them for storage. When the case has done its job for the day the gun should be removed and the case opened to allow any collected moisture to evaporate. Leather cases and the leather trim on soft cases should be treated a couple times a year with Neatsfoot Oil or liquid silicone (refer to the manufacturer as to which) as described in the sling section. The outer surface of cloth cases can be sprayed with fabric water repellant to improve water resistance but bear in mind that reduces its ability to breathe.

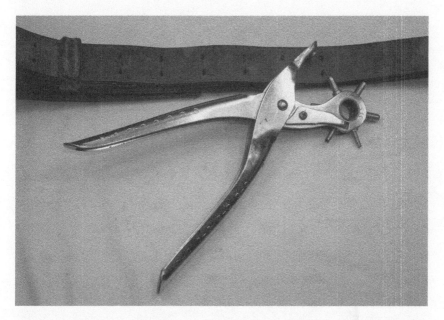

Who hasn't at some time needed an extra hole or two in a gun belt or sling? A hole punch with multiple-sized punches (available from leather-craft stores) is inexpensive and handles any job.

SLING, HOLSTER, AND GUN CASE REPAIR

The most common problem encountered with these leather and cloth accoutrements is stitching failure. Typically, a section of stitching becomes damaged and the broken thread begins to unravel, getting worse as time goes by. If noticed when only a few stitches have come loose the thread can simply be anchored with epoxy to prevent further unraveling. The quick-set version is strong enough for this job. Mix up a small batch and use a toothpick to apply the epoxy to the last two or three stitches that are still intact at each end of the damaged area. Apply the epoxy both front and back and work it down into the stitch holes as well. When the epoxy has set, trim the thread ends.

If a larger area is involved the material will have to be resewn. The materials we're working with are way too heavy for the

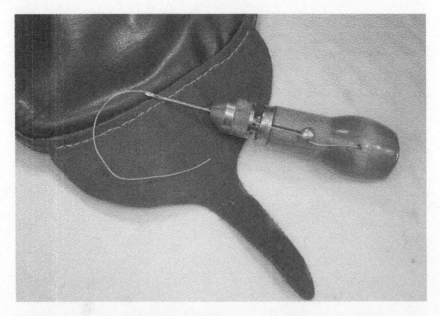

The most common cause of death of leather items is damaged stitching that just keeps unraveling. A sewing awl has many uses from salvage projects to customizing, such as adding this flap to a leather gun case.

little-lady's sewing machine so we'll have to do it ourselves with an awl. These nifty little hand tools allow you to sew professional lock stitches just like a sewing machine. They're available at some craft stores or by mail order from leather-craft supply firms such as the Tandy Company. The thread normally supplied with the awl is much heavier than that typically used on gun cases and such, so it won't perfectly match but you'll never have to worry about it breaking in your lifetime.

Follow the instructions that come with the tool and simply stitch through the existing holes. If the material is cloth you may not be able to see the old stitch holes. In that event, measure the length of the individual stitches of the original stitching and duplicate that with your new stitches. Mark each stitch location with a ruler and pencil to ensure uniform, straight stitching. If

Though a slow, mundane process, using a sewing awl makes professional lock stitching every bit as good as commercial sewing machines do.

the original stitching is very small you may have to make your spacing a bit longer to accommodate the larger needle and thread of the awl. Start and end the sewing several stitches back on the intact stitching so the overlap anchors the loose ends of the original thread. For additional security epoxy the loose thread ends as previously described.

Of course, the awl opens the door for all manner of repair and modifications of leather and cloth items. Sling swivels and belt buckles can be permanently attached by running the sling or belt through the loop, doubling it back on itself and sewing it. A soft or non-slip shoulder pad can be sewn to a sling. Straps or buckles can be added to gun cases.

Should the need arise to cut leather, say for shortening a sling or holster belt, it is best done with a very sharp hobby knife. Keep long cuts straight by running the knife along a metal straightedge. After the cut is made, round the sharp edges of the

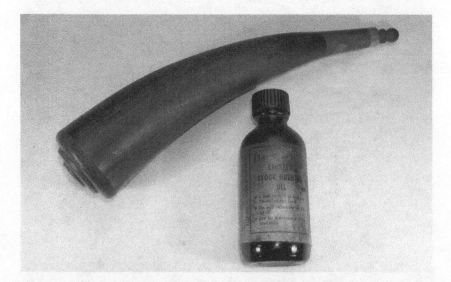

Powderhorns, this one made of bison horn, must be oiled occasionally to prevent them from drying out and cracking. Use gunstock-grade linseed oil and rub it in thoroughly with your hand. Let it soak up all it will but don't allow oil to build up on the surface.

leather with fine sandpaper. Leather can be stained with leather dye available at shoe stores but I don't recommend it. Every dye I've tried leeches out when it gets wet, making a permanent stain on clothes.

A sharp pair of scissors usually works best for cutting cloth material. If the cloth is very thick use sharp tin snips. To prevent thick nylon such as used on slings and belts from unraveling, lightly melt the edge with the open flame of a candle or lighter. While the nylon is still molten, thoroughly wet your fingers and squeeze down any ridges or sharp edges. For this, you'll have to work quickly because the melted nylon turns hard fast. Be sure your fingers are good and wet to keep the molten nylon from sticking to them and scorching your hide.

Chapter 14

FIREARM STORAGE

It may seem obvious, but the first step towards proper firearm storage is to define what we expect to accomplish. We must keep them free of rust. They should be out of the way and inaccessible to children and other uninvited handling. It would also be nice to secure them from damage, fire, and theft.

PREPARATION FOR STORAGE

Procedures for thorough cleaning, oiling, and application of rust preventive are detailed in the advanced-cleaning sections of the individual chapters on gun cleaning. Prior to being stashed away for the off season your guns should receive this attention. You may also want to increase bore protection from rust by applying a heavy coat of grease to the bore. This is especially applicable if the guns are not stored in a climate controlled area with heating and air conditioning. Whenever grease or rust preventive is applied to the bore, stick a reminder note in the action to remove it before firing. Firing the gun with the bore so obstructed would be extremely dangerous. Even if you're confident you will remember, it's always possible someone else could get their hands on it and shoot it.

An exception to the above is if the gun is to serve for home defense. Typically, such a gun sits for months or years without so much as the action being cycled. Over time, dust makes its way inside and lubricants solidify. Despite our intentions of tending to the gun every few months it ain't gonna happen. It's out of sight and out of mind and will likely stay that way until that one dreadful night comes along. Such a gun should be cleaned and critical areas that would normally be oiled can be either lightly lubed with dry graphite or left completely bare. Non-bearing metal surfaces can be protected against rust with rust preventive.

STORAGE METHODS

How we choose to store our firearms depends a lot on how many guns we have and their value. It wouldn't make much sense to buy a two-thousand-dollar gun safe to store only a few guns with a combined value of something less. On the flip side, it's pretty stupid to have a firearm collection worth many thousands of dollars and not do all you can to prevent it from going up in smoke or funding some burglar's drug habit.

Obviously, a gun safe is far and away the best way to store firearms. The average person worries about theft but an equal, if not greater, threat to our guns is fire. With a safe, fire, theft, and other uninvited access all become non-issues. When buying a safe it's good sense to spring for one large enough to accommodate not only your current firearm inventory, but future acquisitions, as well. Of course, an alternative would be to get two, though that would require considerably more cash. And what about those of us who have so many guns it would take a vault bigger than Fort Knox? Obviously, we get the biggest safe feasible for our most prized guns and go to plan B for those of lesser value.

The standard storage system for our fathers and grandfathers was the glass-fronted gun cabinet. Everyone loves to show off their guns and these fine pieces of cabinetry standing proudly in

Anyone with a valuable collection of firearms is crazy not to invest in a gun safe. It's the ultimate protection from theft, fire, and uninvited access.

Gun cabinets were once highly regarded for firearm storage. It is a classy way to store firearms but having them on display invites theft, from which even the best of cabinets afford only limited protection.

the living room or den were the perfect forum. Those times are gone, though. Nowadays that would be like putting a neon sign in the front yard saying, "Free guns, come on in." A gun cabinet can still provide useful storage but it should be out of sight not only from passersby but from visitors. Who knows when one of Junior's buddies or a furnace repairman might decide he needs those guns more than you do? Since displaying the guns is not the goal, the cabinet might just as well be a hell-for-stout plywood box with solid doors and a sturdy lock and hinges. For extra security bolt it to the wall. This can be made for a reasonable price by anyone with a modicum of carpenter skills. Of course, it's useless

Gun racks are simply a convenient place to prop guns, affording no protection from anything. A padlocked cable running through the trigger guards would provide modest theft protection. Note the guns with recoil pads are stored muzzle down to prevent crushing of the pads.

against a house fire and someone with enough time and wrecking tools could eventually make their way in, but it's a whole lot better than simply standing the guns in various corners.

Then there's the venerable floor gun rack. These are popular because they store a lot of guns in a small amount of space at very little expense. Unfortunately, they're just a handy place to lean a gun and afford no protection from anything. A padlocked chain or cable situated to run through the trigger guards can be installed to provide modest theft protection and a sheet thrown over the whole works keeps the dust off. The same applies to wall gun racks where guns are stored horizontally on the wall.

Action locks (top) or trigger locks (bottom) prevent unauthorized people from using the gun. They are a must in households with inquisitive children or irresponsible family members.

Of course, all manner of ingenious storage methods have been devised. False walls are popular as are closets faced off to blend into the surrounding walls. These may secure them from unwanted eyes but, again, they provide no fire protection. With any system other than a fireproof gun safe, I prefer the guns to be quickly accessible so they can be pitched out the window should fire threaten.

Though a pain in the butt, trigger locks are a good idea no matter how secure you think your guns may be. Not only do they provide the obvious kid proofing, they offer a certain sense of satisfaction should your guns be stolen. The thief will eventually get them off one way or another but he'll likely damage the gun in the process, reducing their black-market value. On the other hand, he may figure it's not worth the effort and abandon the guns, enhancing the chance of recovery.

Whatever storage system you decide on be sure it's located where temperature and humidity are relatively stable. Damp areas such as basements are the kiss of death. Rust quickly appears, stocks take on moisture and mold forms on slings. Hot, stuffy attics can severely dry out wooden stocks and slings. Continual temperature and humidity changes cause wood to shrink and swell which can loosen the finish. If you are using a gun safe or enclosed cabinet there are small air dryers available for around fifty bucks that keep the air inside warm and dry. An alternative is to use a desiccant material such as silica gel inside the enclosure to absorb moisture. This can be re-used over and over by drying it out in the oven.

You've surely noticed on many older guns that the recoil pads are smooshed down at the heel. That's from a lifetime of the gun sitting butt down with the full weight bearing on the pad. The extra-soft pads now available are especially susceptible

A dehumidifier or a moisture-absorbing agent such as this desiccant in an enclosed storage unit such as a safe or gun cabinet greatly reduces rusting problems.

to this and can show signs of flattening in just a few months. If at all possible, store guns equipped with recoil pads muzzle down or horizontally. If they must be stored butt down insert a dowel or similar object into the pad screw hole to support the weight of the gun.

Another consideration for long term storage is to reduce the tension on the mainspring and certain other action springs whenever possible. In reality, springs that are well designed and properly tempered should hold up to living under full tension indefinitely. However, why not make their lives easier by storing the gun with the action in the fired position? Any respectable centerfire gun, whether rifle, handgun, or shotgun, should withstand being fired with an empty chamber on occasion. This subjects

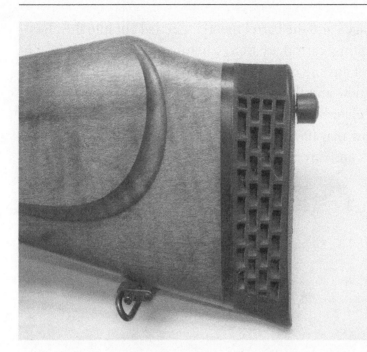

When continually stored butt down, recoil pads can become squashed out. Some manufacturers provide a support pin with their extra-soft pads that is inserted in the screw hole to support the weight of the gun. A piece of wood dowel serves the same purpose.

the firing pin to a certain amount of stress but it shouldn't cause any problems. If you're concerned about it, as many folks are, order some snap caps. These are essentially dummy cartridges, usually made of plastic, and provide resistance to the firing-pin fall like a real cartridge. Shotgun snap caps are quite common. Harder to find are snap caps for rifle and handgun cartridges. You'll likely have to turn to a gunsmith supplier for these. You don't need the fancy practice dummy rounds with spring-loaded primers, just plain old snap caps.

It's an entirely different story with rimfires. *Never, ever dry fire a rimfire.* The firing pin is aligned to hit on the outer rim of the cartridge so when the firing pin falls with the chamber empty it slams into the back edge of the barrel. In short order the firing pin is damaged and the barrel metal is peened out into the chamber, preventing cartridges from chambering. Surprisingly, I'm not aware of anyone offering rimfire snap caps. Since we're only doing this now and then, just save a few fired casings and insert one in the chamber whenever you dry fire the gun. Note that the empty casing may have to be one fired by that gun because chamber dimensions vary slightly and one from another gun may be too large.

Chapter 15

TROUBLESHOOTING

Guns being the mechanical things that they are, it's inevitable they will malfunction on occasion. In most cases this will require a trip to the local 'smitty but if the affliction is minor we may be able to fix it ourselves and save a few bucks. It's beyond the scope of this book to go into broken-part repair but if you're thinking of trying it I'll throw out this tip—it's usually more time- and cost-effective to replace the part rather than trying to fix it. The Gun Parts Corporation carries a huge inventory of replacement parts, particularly for older guns. Brownell's has a fair inventory of new gun parts and, of course, you can often get parts from the factory or importer. Replacing an obviously broken part is pretty straightforward. Determining what's causing a given problem, though, is often the biggest challenge. Here are a few tips on dealing with some of the more common gun ailments.

MISFIRES

Any number of things can cause a gun not to go bang. If it just all of a sudden quits and refuses to fire no matter what, either a part broke or some foreign object is blocking a critical mechanism. First check the primer of the cartridge. If it has a deep, full dent similar to other fired primers, the problem is with the ammo. That, however, is a very rare occurrence. If there is no firing pin dent in the primer or if it's less dented than a normal fired one, check the firing-pin tip. It should be well formed and nicely rounded (or neatly squared off if a rimfire). If it's jagged or otherwise deformed, that's likely the culprit.

If the firing pin looks okay the next check is the mainspring that drives the firing pin. That will require getting into the bolt or guts of the action, depending on the gun type. Handgun mainsprings lie under the grips. If the mainspring is still intact, while you're in there look for a metal shaving, weed seed, or any foreign object that could be preventing the firing pin from completely falling. From here on, the detective work gets tougher. You can root around in the action looking for something broken but it's probably time to call on your trusty gunsmith.

A different scenario is if the misfires are sporadic, the gun sometimes firing, sometimes not. Again, compare the dent in the misfired primer with the dent in a fired one from another gun. If the misfired primer has a noticeably weaker dent that means either the firing pin isn't giving it a good whack or the ammo has exceptionally hard primers. I've never encountered primer problems with name-brand ammo or reloads using name-brand primers. However, bargain-special ammo or reload primers from an unfamiliar manufacturer in some obscure Third World country could be suspect.

Most likely we'll have to search on. The most common cause of sporadic misfires is the firing pin being worn or peened back. Inspect the firing pin tip to see if it's slightly flattened or bulged at the tip. This requires replacement of the firing pin. It's possible the mainspring that drives the firing pin has weakened. Though it seems like this should be a common problem it seldom is. Usually a spring is either good for the duration or fails completely at birth. If it's a leaf or "V" spring, look closely for a crack, especially near the base of the "V." If all these things pass inspection look for dirty, gummed up parts or errant metal shavings that could be hindering proper function.

STICKY, HARD WORKING ACTION

A well-made gun is supposed to cycle smoothly and effortlessly. If not, something's obviously wrong. The most common cause, especially with a gun that hasn't been used in a long time is old, gummy lubricant, perhaps assisted by a build-up of powder residue and a coating of dust. Even if the gun has seen recent action, start with a thorough cleaning. If nothing else that will clear the way for further inspection. While cleaning, look for metal shavings or other foreign matter that could be hampering free movement. Also check for protruding metal burrs. These can be filed off or carefully removed with a hand grinder. Just be sure to not alter any critical shapes or dimensions.

If the gun is scoped, check the scope-mount screws to make sure they're not protruding below the receiver wall and binding the bolt or other parts. A loosened screw or pin within the action

Rough, balky actions can be smoothed with action-honing stones and/or a polishing compound. Twelve time national pistol champion Eric Weeldryer commonly uses J-B bore cleaner for this.

could be binding on something or allowing the part it holds to misalign and bind. Similarly, a broken, non-critical part that has so far gone unnoticed could be binding things up. I routinely encounter all of these malfunctions.

CARTRIDGE STICKING IN CHAMBER—RIFLES AND HANDGUNS

This one strikes fear into knowledgeable shooters' hearts as it can be a sign of pressure elevated into the health-hazard range. With luck you were able to get the action open and the cartridge extracted. If the gun is a bolt rifle you can do a little judicious whacking on the bolt handle with a piece of wood if necessary. Don't get crazy, though. With some guns such as the Remington 700 the bolt handle is silver soldered on rather than an integral part of the bolt and too much gusto with the wood can break the bolt handle off. It's also possible to bend the bolt handle. If you can't get the action open with only moderate force take it to the

Primer shape can be a good indicator of excessive pressure. The one at left is normal. The primer at right is flattened which is a sure sign of pressure beyond acceptable limits.

gunsmith. If the action opens but the cartridge remains stuck in the chamber it can usually be driven out with a wood or brass rod inserted down the muzzle. For extreme cases, remove the stock and spray a copious amount of penetrating lubricant such as Liquid Wrench or WD-40 down the bore and stand the action muzzle up to soak a few hours.

Once the cartridge is out, inspect the primer. The outer perimeter of the primer should have a slight bevel all the way around. If the primer is flatter than a pancake with no hint of a bevel, pressure was too high. If in addition to this, there's a slight, raised crater rim around the firing-pin dent, pressure was scary high. Inspect the base of the cartridge. If there's a bright, shiny, burnished area, that also suggests extreme pressure. Determining if pressure was a factor is the easy part. Finding the cause can involve a lot of frustrating detective work.

First we'll take the scenario where suddenly a cartridge sticks in a gun that you know had previously worked fine. Guns don't just all of a sudden start misbehaving on their own. They don't change chamber or bore dimensions in the dark of night. If it has no prior history of creating high pressure the gun is undeniably innocent. The problem has to lie elsewhere.

The first thing to consider is if there could have been an obstruction in the bore when the shot was fired. This could be anything from grease or large amounts of rust preventive to some object that somehow made its way in there. I make it a habit to always visually check the bore before heading to the range or afield to avoid such problems. If obstruction was a possibility, keep it in mind but don't fire another round to see if things improve. There's too much chance of damaging the gun and yourself. We'll explore other possibilities first.

If the round was a reload, suspicions go to an improper powder charge. We all know too much powder is not good. Lesser known is that too little powder can also cause high pressure. Gun powder is supposed to rapidly burn, not explode all at once. Certain powders in too small a quantity in certain cartridges can actually detonate like a bomb rather than burn which sends pressure into the ozone. Disassemble all the remaining cartridges and weigh the powder charges. If they are all hunky-dory, check the load recipe you used with several different manuals. Some manuals may list a higher powder charge than others. Some guns are pressure sensitive due to a tight chamber, tight bore, or a combination of both. Such a gun may not be able to safely handle as much powder as a given manual's test gun. This is more common than most folks realize. I once had a commercially made, 7x57 Mauser that couldn't even handle listed starting loads, much less anything toward maximum.

I'll also remind you that the given load recipe must be followed exactly. Any change in casing brand, primer, bullet weight, or shape can significantly raise pressure. Be sure casings do not exceed maximum length which can cause problems. If the recipe checks out, measure the bullets with a micrometer or calipers to ensure they are the proper size. Also check the depth the bullet is seated. If the bullet is not set deep enough it could bear tightly on the lands of the rifling when chambered which significantly raises pressure. Along these lines, never shoot someone else's reloads. What works fine in their gun may not in yours. Then, too, he may have been swilling "Old Stump Blower" and been on the wrong page of the reloading manual.

Was the powder reasonably fresh or older than your grandmother? One time I had a disturbing experience with my cherished buddy, a Ruger .22-250 Varminter. It had always digested my pet load without complaint but after a winter layoff the pressure of the first shot jumped so high it blew the primer completely out of the casing and forged the case head back around the bolt nose. If the gun had been of lesser character than the famously stout Ruger it probably would have come apart at the seams. I cut the powder charge way back and it still showed signs of extreme pressure. For weeks I wracked my brains and checked and rechecked everything without finding a cause. Finally I broke down and bought a new can of powder. The problem disappeared. I knew the powder I had previously used was old but it looked and smelled fine. Normally, deteriorating powder loses strength but in researching I found that some powders can become extremely volatile in the early stages of deterioration.

Finally, if your load was close to maximum and the cartridges were superheated, such as having sat on the dashboard with a hot sun beating down through the windshield, that could cause pressure problems.

If the cartridge was a name-brand factory load and reasonably new it's a good bet it's not a cartridge problem. Reputable factories just don't screw up and they don't use loads that push the pressure envelope. I shouldn't have to say it, but I guess I'd better mention to make sure the cartridge was the right one for the gun. I've had several guns come into the shop with the remains of a wrong cartridge scattered throughout its innards.

If the cartridges have proven innocent, and we already know the gun to be innocent, the only suspect left is some form of bore obstruction. Give the bore a good cleaning and head to some desolate area with a safe backstop where no one is around. Our momma raised no idiots so for this test we'll securely lash the gun into a tire (padded with a towel, of course) with the muzzle of the gun pointed into the nearby backstop. Be sure there is no possibility of a ricochet and that no one could come along unnoticed. Tie a long string onto the trigger and take cover behind a substantial wall, building, or big tree. Yank the string and when the smoke clears check the results. All should be well but try a few more shots from cover just to be sure. As a final ammo check, start with new factory loads and then try some from the same batch that stuck.

A trickier scenario is when the gun is new to you. Since you don't know its prior history, the gun is now equally suspect of all the previously mentioned infractions. One thing that can be devastating is the gun having been rechambered to some other cartridge than what's stamped on the barrel. The true chambering can be determined by making a sulphur cast of the chamber and taking measurements from it. That's pretty much gunsmith territory, though.

Though extremely rare, the bore could be undersized. I once made a fine custom rifle in .243 Winchester for a friend of mine. The barreled action he supplied was a highly renowned Mauser Sporter. Upon the first test shot of the finished masterpiece the casing stuck tightly in the chamber. After being beaten out, the casing displayed all the signs of pressure going stratospheric. I checked everything again and again but could not find the problem. Finally I slugged the bore. This is done by driving a soft lead slug through the bore and then measuring it. I was dumbfounded to find the supposedly .243 was actually a .239, four-thousandths of an inch undersized! From the stampings it was obvious the barrel came from the Mauser factory. They had apparently used a reamer that had been sharpened too many times and was severely undersized. I salvaged the gun with the long and tedious process of enlarging the bore by hand lapping with cast-lead laps.

The final gun anomaly that can cause dangerous conditions is too much headspace. That simply means the chamber is too long and the casing stretches an inordinate amount upon firing. The casing may even crack or completely separate, usually near the base. Excessive headspace is caused by either the barrel not being fully seated in the action or the chamber being cut too long. Headspace can be checked with a special no-go headspace gauge. It would be highly unusual to encounter this in a factory built gun but is not uncommon in custom, rechambered, or re-barreled firearms.

Checking any or all of these conditions is probably best left to a gunsmith. The materials and tools are readily available from gunsmith-supply firms but it takes a certain amount of expertise to use them and the expense of the tools may not warrant fooling with it yourself.

If a stuck casing does not show signs of excessive pressure several other things could be coming into play. Check the extractor to be sure it is not worn or broken and that it is under enough spring tension to grip the cartridge rim firmly. Also be sure the chamber and cartridge were clean. A heavy build-up of residue in the chamber or grit or other foreign matter on the casing could cause a cartridge to bind.

A rough chamber is best smoothed by lapping with a brass casing and polishing compound. The casing must be fired from that gun to ensure precise fit. A rod soldered into the primer pocket allows the lap to be turned with a hand drill.

If the problem has been ongoing perhaps the chamber is rough or rusted. If so, a good polishing is in order. We can do this ourselves if it's a bolt action or other action where the chamber is accessible from the rear (if the action type does not allow access, the barrel will have to be removed; again, time to call on your gunsmith). We'll use an empty casing coated with polishing compound and driven by an electric hand drill. Remove the primer from three empty brass casings (not nickel plated) that have been fired in that gun. They must be fired from that gun so the casings fit the chamber perfectly. If you don't have reloading equipment simply use a small punch to knock out the primers. Solder a length of coat hanger or similar wire into the primer hole of each casing, making it as straight as possible. The wire must be long enough to extend a short ways beyond the rear of the action.

Clean the chamber well. Coat the body and neck of one of the casings with 400-grit paste polishing compound. Don't put compound on the shoulder (or belt if the case is a belted magnum). Cartridges headspace on the shoulder (or belt with belted magnums) and removing metal here could cause headspace problems. Carefully insert the cartridge into the chamber and check the wire in the drill. While exerting only enough forward pressure to ensure the casing is fully seated, run the drill at high speed for about six seconds. We're not trying to remove tool marks or deep rust pits. That would enlarge the chamber too much. We just want to take the curse off rough edges or remove surface rust. Thoroughly clean the chamber and repeat the process with another casing and 600-grit compound. After cleaning, coat the third casing with a fine polishing compound such as jeweler's rouge or aluminum-oxide polishing compound. This time run the drill about ten seconds—the polishing compound won't remove any measurable amount of metal.

Dry firing rimfire guns deforms the rear of the chamber. Restore to shape by carefully filing with a fine-toothed, round jeweler's file.

Thoroughly clean the chamber and bore, reassemble the gun, and the job's done.

The cause of stuck casings in rimfires is most often due to the chamber being deformed at the very rear from dry firing. As mentioned earlier, with no cartridge rim to block the firing pin, the pin hits the edge of the barrel with great force. Repeatedly doing this peens the rear of the chamber out of shape. If the damage is significant enough to cause feeding and ejection problems, a lump extending into the chamber can be seen with the naked eye. Carefully file this off with a fine-toothed, round needle file. Don't overdo it; just bring the chamber back into round. Polish the file marks with a tiny piece of 600-grit sandpaper wrapped around a small dowel.

CARTRIDGE STICKING IN CHAMBER—SHOTGUNS

With shotguns our diagnosis is hampered because a shotgun shell shows no signs of high pressure no matter how bad it gets. Be sure the chamber was clean when the shot was fired. An exceptionally rough or rusted chamber can cause casings to stick. Smooth and polish shotgun chambers with wet-or-dry sandpaper wrapped around a bronze bore-cleaning brush. Cut pieces of sandpaper the width of the brush and long enough to wrap completely around the brush. Screw the brush into the tip section of a take-down cleaning rod and turn the rod with an electric drill. Use cutting oil on the sandpaper and keep the paper moving evenly back and forth in the chamber. Wrap the paper around the brush counterclockwise (looking from rear) and friction should hold it in place on the brush. If not, secure it with a small piece of duct tape, then wrap. We're not trying to remove tool marks, just smooth things up a bit. Start with 400 grit and only sand at slow speed about five seconds. Clean the chamber, switch to 600 grit and sand, again at slow speed, for about eight seconds. That should do it.

Check the extractor to be sure it isn't damaged or worn and that it is functioning properly. Again, since we can't tell if pressure was the culprit we're pretty much running blind. If none of the above appear to be causing the problem it's best to take it to a gunsmith for a complete diagnosis.

FAILURE TO FEED

Cartridge feeding problems seldom occur in factory built bolt actions. On rare occasions a particular gun may have trouble with long, blunt, round-nosed bullets. Improperly reloaded ammo can cause feeding problems. Exceptionally long or improperly seated bullets may cause issues as can over-length casings that have not

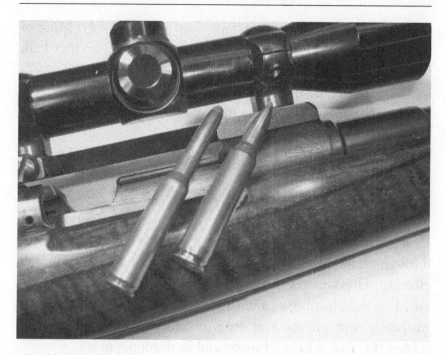

Long, blunt-nosed bullets, such as the one at left, or bullets incorrectly seated, is a common cause of feeding problems.

been trimmed back within tolerance. A casing that has been fired in another gun with a slightly larger chamber and then only neck sized during reloading will not chamber.

Some bolt action rimfires employ tubular magazines which then require a feeding mechanism to transport the cartridge from the magazine and align it with the chamber. Something within this mechanism could be broken or the whole works simply bogged down with crud and debris. Detachable magazines can be persnickety. If you suspect this to be a problem try another one. For box magazines, be sure the cartridge follower is not installed backwards. If the gun has been rechambered to a different cartridge, especially one significantly larger than the original, the feed-ramp configuration may need to be changed. This is another job for a gunsmith.

Pumps and lever actions also feed quite reliably. Most of these are designed for round-nosed bullets and the gun may balk if fed flat-nosed wadcutter or semi-wadcutter bullets or other bullets of unusual design. Assuming the innards are reasonably clean, any failure other than that is likely caused by a broken part, which calls for the attention of a gunsmith.

While bolt, pump, and lever guns are relatively trouble free, it seems semi-autos are just begging for an excuse to jam. The biggest culprit is poor hygiene. Gas-operated versions like the Remington 1100 can be especially finicky, requiring very regular cleaning of the gas system. I've seen some that can't even make it through an afternoon of trap shooting without a seventh-inning cleanup. Don't forget the gas ports in the barrel. Clean as detailed in the cleaning chapter for those guns. Be sure the steel gas-piston ring and gas seal are installed correctly and that the rubber "O" ring is in good shape and in its proper place.

Some semi-auto shotguns may have trouble digesting either really heavy or really light loads. For instance, a gun designed for trap or skeet often jams with heavy game loads. The reverse holds true for heavy-duty hunting guns—they may not handle target loads. Some, such as the venerable Browning Auto-5, compensate for load differences by the positioning of the compression ring or similar part. It's placed in front of the recoil spring for heavy loads and stored behind the spring for light loads.

Semi-auto rimfire rifles can be temperamental. Of course, nearly all .22 semi-autos will only handle long-rifle cartridges. They don't even try to work with longs or shorts. Some may not work well with the extra hot loadings like Stingers or those with unusual bullet-nose designs. They should be squeaky clean inside and properly lubed so the parts work freely. One gun warranting particular note because it is so popular is the Marlin Model 60 and its various versions. In the innards is a unit called the feed-throat assembly and when this unit goes bad, which it notoriously does, the whole thing must be replaced. This is an assignment for a gunsmith (who mostly likely has a bucket full of replacements on hand).

Semi-auto handguns typically cause the most frustrations. The worst offenders are inexpensive self-defense type pistols but any of them can have their demented moments. Of course, the gun must be clean and properly lubed. Many are sensitive to bullet-nose shape, power level of the cartridge, or both. You may have to try a variety of ammo brands and loads to find those that function reliably. The other common cause of feeding failure in these guns is the magazine lips. They have to be at just the right angle. There are no rules here, you just bend them in or out a tiny bit at a time by trial and error. Use a pair of pliers padded with leather. Particularly obstinate magazines deserve a place in the trash can if replacements are available.

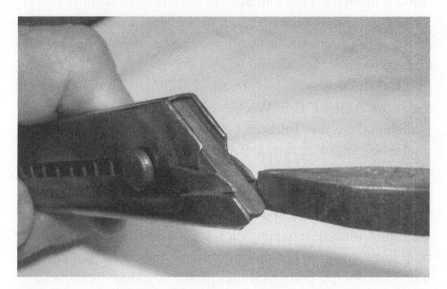

Magazines can be a source of feeding problems, especially in semi-auto handguns. If bullet shape is not the problem try adjusting the angle of the magazine lips. It's strictly trial and error and go just a tiny bit at a time. Smooth-jawed pliers prevent damage to the magazine.

Balky, stiff-working slides can enter into the picture, too. If the cause is crud and gummed lubricant a simple cleaning takes care of things. If it's burrs or rough machining, some polishing is in order. This can be done in two ways, either by hand stoning or applying polishing compound to the slide and corresponding areas of the frame and barrel and working the slide back and forth for as long as it takes to smooth things up. For stoning, a set of fine action-honing stones is required. This includes a variety of stone shapes, some or all of which may best do a given portion of the job. Always use plenty of whetstone oil on the stones to keep them from clogging. Simply look for protruding burrs and bright, shiny areas on the slide, frame, barrel, and any other places that contact each other. Burrs, if really prominent, can first be filed down then polished with the stones. Rough-machined areas should be just lightly stoned to smooth them up. Don't attempt to remove the machine marks. That would likely take off too much metal. Take great care to run the stones evenly without rocking to keep corners sharp and contours as they should be.

If the problem isn't severe, the polishing-compound route is the better method. Eric Weeldryer, twelve time National handgun champion, says J-B Bore Cleaner is the best polishing compound he's found for this (and also why he never uses J-B for bore cleaning). If there are some exceptionally rough areas, lightly stone them first or you'll make a career out of knocking them down with the fine compound. Apply compound to all the shiny areas that indicate contact, stick a good DVD into the player, pour three fingers of top-shelf scotch (all right, make it ginger ale while handling a gun), and commence working the slide back and forth. When things seem sufficiently loosened up, be sure to remove every last bit of compound before assembly.

FAILURE TO EJECT

With the exception of semi-autos, cartridge-ejection problems are pretty straightforward. In the vast majority of cases the cause is a broken ejector or ejector spring. In bolt actions the ejector is either a mechanism at the rear of the action or a little plunger in the face of the bolt. It's quite easy to determine if a part is broken or missing. Check the spring by manually working the ejector in and out to see if it's under proper tension. On break-actions equipped with ejectors, the ejectors and springs are usually visible on the bottom side of the barrels. Ejector styles differ greatly on the various models of pump, semi-auto, and lever guns but it's most always a part on the inside attached to the side of the action that hits the rim of the casing as the bolt cycles rearward, kicking the casing out.

If a three-inch shotgun shell is fired in a pump or semi-auto shotgun chambered for two-and-three-quarter-inch cartridges (which, by the way, can be very hazardous to your health), the longer casing will hang up in the ejection port. Sometimes a very low-mounted scope on a bolt action can cause problems. The cartridge flips upward, hits the scope, and falls back into the action.

As previously discussed in the feeding section, semi-autos, whether rifle, shotgun, or pistol, can be finicky as to cartridge power. If the gun is designed for heavy loads, a light target round may not have the oomph to properly cycle the action. In the reverse, a magnum or heavy game load fired in a gun designed for light target ammo may cycle the action so fast and hard that things can't keep up and the casing is caught inside the action. Semi-autos must be kept clean and freshly lubed. Powder residue and old, petrified lubricant can slow the action down enough that the casing won't eject.

POOR ACCURACY

Before we can discuss accuracy problems we must first make sure our expectations are reasonable. Rarely does a week go by without someone asking me about their sick gun that just doesn't shoot like it's supposed to. "What kind of gun," I query? "A Rem-Chester bolt action, .30-'06," they reply. "And what group size are you getting at a hundred yards," I ask. They hold up their hands forming a two- or three-inch circle. Well, for the average shooter with an average hunting rifle, factory ammo, and shooting from some makeshift rest at best, that ain't bad. The gun magazines have filled our heads with tales of half-, three-quarter, and one-inch groups but that is not typical.

There are so many variables in the accuracy equation that it's hard to define how well a given gun should shoot. To talk potential accuracy we must assume a number of givens are in place. The ammo must be inherently accurate and the bullet weight compatible with the gun's rifling twist. Factory guns of a given caliber usually shoot their best with bullet weights in the mid-range of the spectrum. For example, a typical .30-'06 will shoot best with bullets in the 150- to 180-grain range. Bullets as light as 110-grains and as heavy as 220-grains are commonly available but the farther we get from the mid-point the less likely the gun will like them. On the other hand, a .300 Magnum, though quite similar to the .30-'06, is designed for bigger game and will probably shoot 180- to 200-grain bullets better. There are exceptions of course, but the first step toward accuracy is finding the right bullet weight for a particular gun.

For shotgun-slug shooters, know that the whiz-bang saboted slugs now so popular only work well in rifled barrels. With a smoothbore you'll be lucky to hit the one-hundred-yard bunker, much less the target. The standard Foster-style slugs are the

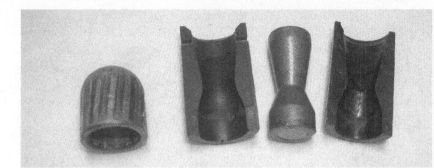

The standard Foster-style slug is the most accurate from smoothbore shotguns. Saboted slugs (right) are for use in rifled-barreled shotguns.

fodder for smoothbores. Similarly for muzzle-loaders, saboted bullets require a fast rifling twist to stabilize the bullet while long, heavy bullets and roundballs insist on a slow twist. Guns designed for long bullets and roundballs won't shoot sabots for beans and vice versa.

Until recently, standard factory ammo was notoriously poor shooting. A knowledgeable handloader could most always concoct ammo that would shoot rings around the factory stuff. It took over a century but commercial ammo makers finally realized serious shooters are willing to pay for good ammunition. Today's premium ammo will usually shoot right along with the best of reloads. If performance is the game, lay out the extra cash for premium ammo. It makes sense to practice with standard ammo but don't use it to measure your guns' accuracy potential.

Another thing to consider is the sighting equipment. Do not expect to shoot tight groups at long distances with open sights or low-power scopes. It just ain't gonna happen. Not all scopes are equal, either. The more magnification and finer crosshairs we have the greater the accuracy potential. Broad crosshairs can cover several inches of target at one hundred yards. It's a tall order to try and shoot one-inch groups when the crosshairs cover

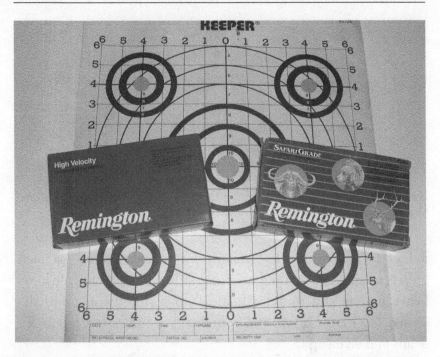

Standard ammunition (left) is fine for practice and close-range hunting. Premium ammo (right) is usually more accurate.

three inches of the target. That's not to say a ridiculously high-powered target scope belongs on a general hunting rifle, just don't compare a gun set up for hunting with one decked out for target shooting or varminting.

Now comes the brutal truth that the gun scribes don't talk about. The biggest factor in the accuracy equation is the shooter. Quite frankly, Average Joe Buck Slayer who only drags his gun out of mothballs for deer season probably can't shoot for snot. Typically he flinches like a gun-shy mule and has not a clue of even the most basic shooting fundamentals. Even casual shooters rarely measure up to anywhere near the gun's potential. I dread it when Joe Buck Slayer commandeers me to fix his ill shooting gun for him. Not that I'm a great shot, but the cure is usually an embarrassing trip to the range where the gun somehow magically shoots a respectable group. When going for accuracy you have to do your part. Employ a rock solid bench, good sandbags, and know and exercise all the shooting fundamentals as described in the scope sighting section.

All that said, now I will tread into perilous waters and tell you what I consider typical accuracy expectations. I'm assuming all the above givens are in place, accurate ammo with bullets of the gun's preference, a scope with fair magnification, typical duplex crosshairs, and a good shot at the helm. I'm talking five-shot groups at one-hundred yards, excepting handguns and .22 rimfires which we'll measure at fifty yards. I'll also discount the occasional flyer, which may or may not be human error.

I'm happy if a typical centerfire bolt action shoots one-and-a-half-inch groups and I'll accept two-inch. Modern centerfire pumps and semi-autos have improved in accuracy and a few will take on a bolt rifle any day. Taking the breed as a whole, though, I wouldn't be ashamed of three-inch to four-inch groups. Lever actions are within the acceptance level with four-inch or five-inch groups or a bit more. This is more a matter of the cartridges for which they are typically chambered rather than the guns themselves. Pump and semi-auto shotguns with rifled barrel and saboted slugs typically come in at around three to four inches. With smoothbore barrels and Foster-style slugs, these guns typically group about five to six inches. Bolt action and single-shot shotguns designed specifically for slugs will shock your socks off. Saboted slugs from their rifled barrels should easily group two to three inches and half that is not uncommon. With standard ammo most small-caliber rimfires regardless of action type will group in the neighborhood of two to three inches at fifty yards. Scoped handguns can be expected to group around six inches at fifty yards in the hands of a decent shooter. Those are what I deem reasonable expectations. If yours shoots a tad worse I wouldn't worry about it. If it shoots better, which many will, be happy. If a gun is far off from these averages, though, something is amiss.

Extreme copper or lead build-up can affect accuracy. I once inherited a 6.5 mm Swedish Mauser which I restocked and scoped for a knockaround farm gun. I was disappointed to find four-inch groups was all she could muster. I knew the bore had been casually cleaned more or less regularly but likely no special attention had been paid to copper fouling since the Spanish American War. It took the better part of a day with copper solvent to grub out a pound of copper but after that she'd regularly plunk five shots into a half dollar. An electronic cleaning unit would have saved a ton of time but I didn't have one then. While cleaning, inspect the bore for wear or rust pitting as described in the cleaning section. Obviously loose scope mounts or sight screws aren't conducive to good accuracy so make that one of the first things you check. Also be sure the action screws are tight. With bolt actions always tighten the front screw first, then the rear one. As you tighten the rear screw, lightly place a finger on the rear tang. If you feel the tang move there are action bedding problems. The action screws should also be free in their stock holes with no binding.

There's not much the hobbyist can do mechanically to improve the accuracy of pump, semi-auto, and lever action rifles. You pretty much have what you get. Bolt actions, however, can sometimes be made happier with some attention to the stock bedding. One of the most critical elements of stock bedding from an accuracy standpoint is the barrel bedding.

There are two acceptable ways for bedding a barrel. Highly popular today is a method called free floating. This is where the forend does not touch the barrel beyond just a couple inches in front of the action. Manufacturers love this because they don't have to fiddle around with getting proper forend tension and, if the gap is left big enough, even if a forend warps it will not affect accuracy. This allows them to use wood with less than perfect grain structure in the forend area. It's a common notion that the free-floating barrel is a modern innovation but it has been the accepted way of bedding bull-barreled target rifles for nearly a century. However, despite widespread belief, it's not necessarily the best for lighter sporter barrels.

Virtually from the inception of bolt rifles with one piece stocks, stockmakers have known that some upward pressure on the barrel at the forend tip generally provides better, more consistant accuracy with standard and lightweight barrels. It dampens barrel vibration and barrel whip, both of which increase as the barrel diameter lessens. The amount of upward pressure should be approximately four to five pounds, though I've never found a way to measure that. Some makers apply the pressure from a single point at the bottom of the barrel, others at two points forty-five degrees from center acting like a "V" block to center the barrel and ensure even pressure. For wood stocks with the potential of warping with humidity changes I prefer the former. There's less chance that some slight sideways warping will create uneven pressure, especially if the barrel is properly free floated on each side. With the double-point system the slightest sideways warping will cause uneven pressure. If the stock is synthetic where warping is a non-issue, the double-point system may better dampen vibration and whip.

If the errant shots tend to string out in a diagonal or sideways line, usually upward, as the barrel warms up, that may indicate uneven forend pressure on the barrel. First check the barrel bedding by running a narrow strip of paper between the forend and barrel. If it slides freely the full length it's obviously free floated and pressure isn't the problem. If the paper is stopped at the forend tip, try slipping the paper in further back. Barrel and forend contact should only be at the tip of the forend and just in front of the action.

For a more accurate determination of the amount and location of contact between barrel and forend, remove the stock and coat the entire underside of the barrel with lipstick. Carefully reinstall the stock, taking care that the barrel doesn't contact the forend unnaturally. With the stock again removed the lipstick spots on the forend will clearly portray every point of contact. Remove all these high spots with a barrel-bedding rasp, available from suppliers of gunsmithing tools. In a pinch you can also use

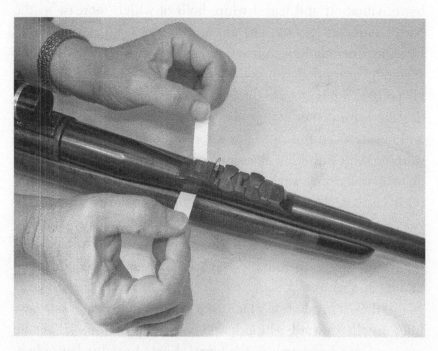

Slide a strip of paper between barrel and forend to determine if there is contact. Sporter barrels typically shoot best with slight upward pressure at the forend tip.

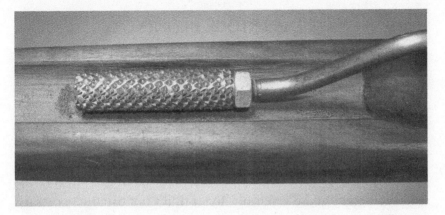

Barrel inletting work is best done with an offset barrel-inletting rasp available from gunsmith-supply firms such as Brownell's.

coarse sandpaper wrapped around a short piece of dowel. It may take several lipstick checks to get them all. Now you have a free-floated barrel. Take the gun to the range and see how she shoots. It's to be hoped that things have improved, especially any tendencies toward shot stringing.

Now let's see the effect some forend pressure can have. Loosen the action screws and slip a narrow shim between the barrel and forend tip to exert slight upward pressure on the bottom of the barrel. Anything will do, a small, folded piece of business card, a piece of your wife's credit card, a cardboard matchstick or two, whatever. Tighten the action screws back up and see how she does now. Fiddle around with the shim thickness between groups to see if more or less pressure makes a difference. If the free-floated barrel shot as well or better and the group was acceptable, great. Pull out the shim and smile. If the group with pressure was significantly better, simply epoxy in a hardwood shim of the same thickness. This can be done with either wood or synthetic stocks.

GLASS STOCK BEDDING

If you're still not satisfied, try glass bedding the entire action. There are a number of bedding compounds on the market. I find Brownell's Acra-Glas Gel to be one of the more user friendly but any of them will certainly do. The game plan is to perfectly bed the rear tang, the front portion of the action, the recoil lug, and about the first two inches of barrel in front of the action. The middle portion of the action we want free floating. I always glass bed the trigger guard assembly, too, but it's not usually necessary.

Disassemble the action, removing all parts such as the trigger, bolt-stop/ejector mechanism, etc. It's imperative there is no reverse draft in any of the metal that would lock the action into

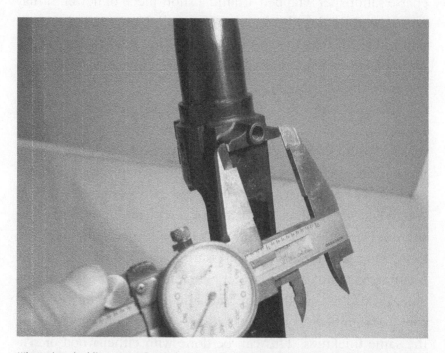

When glass bedding an action it is imperative there are no areas of reverse draft that would permanently lock the action in place. Measure areas such as the recoil lug and tangs to be sure.

the bedding. Carefully inspect the tang and the rest of the action for areas that could cause problems. Measure the recoil lug with a micrometer or calipers to ensure it's not wider at the bottom than the top. File or grind any areas of reverse draft to a slight taper the opposite way to ensure it will easily slip out of the epoxy. Coat the action with lipstick as a spotting compound, install the stock, and then remove it again. Use chisels, rasps, and coarse sandpaper to remove high areas indicated by the lipstick. The only points of contact should be at the rear tang and the very front of the action forward of the recoil lug. Make sure the mortise for the recoil lug is plenty large all the way around and especially at the rear where you want the bedding compound at least an eighth-inch thick.

Fill all holes and crevices (except the action-screw holes) with modeling clay to prevent epoxy getting in. The recoil lug we want in full contact with the bedding at the rear but not the bottom, sides, and front. Perfect clearance can be attained by neatly covering all but the rear of the lug with electrician's tape. When you're absolutely positive there is nothing that could cause the action to be glued permanently in, coat the whole works with the release agent supplied with the bedding compound. Don't forget the action screws, including the heads and screwdriver slots, and their holes. Use plenty of release agent and coat everywhere that could possibly come in contact with the epoxy.

Mix up the bedding compound according to instructions. It takes a certain amount of intuition to know how much compound to put where. You must have enough to completely fill all the voids but you'd prefer that a half-bucketful didn't ooze out on the floor when you sink the action in. Err on the long side, though. Cleaning up some epoxy is much preferable to coming up short. Put goodly amounts of bedding compound everywhere you want it and install the action into the stock. Cinch the action screws good and tight. Using paper towels and pieces of wood as spatulas, clean up all the compound that oozes out. Clamp the gun horizontally level in a vise or similarly prop it up on the bench so the epoxy doesn't run out before it sets. It's now happy hour but I'd sneak back for a peak every ten minutes or so until the epoxy sets to be sure no more excess has seeped out onto unwanted places.

After the bedding compound has cured as recommended it's time to check out your release agent application job. Remove the action screws and gently try to pull the barrel and forend apart. If you can feel the action move you're in luck. The action can then usually be wiggled up out the stock. If that fails, as it probably will, thread in the action screws but leave them a bit short of fully seating. Tap on the heads with a plastic hammer, alternating back and forth between them. You can also apply the hammer to wooden dowels or sticks inserted through the magazine mortise from the bottom to drive the action out. If that's all for naught, spread a bath towel out on the bench top, hold the stock at butt and forend with the barrel horizontal over the padded bench top. Whack the full length of the barrel down on the bench, ensuring that it all hits evenly at the same time. If that didn't work you screwed up. Your last chance is to stuff the gun into the deep freeze overnight. If you're really lucky the metal may shrink enough to break loose from the epoxy. If that doesn't work she's glued in for life unless you chemically dissolve the epoxy, which will destroy synthetic stocks and the finish of wood stocks.

SHOTGUN ACCURACY PROBLEMS

We normally don't think of accuracy issues when sending a swarm of shot downrange but if we're to be decent scattergunners, our guns have to shoot where we're pointing them. The shotgunner's equivalent of a target is the pattern board. Ideally, you have access to a range with a large, steel pattern board that can be greased over to reveal patterns. If not, you'll have to make do with big pieces of cardboard. Place a small aiming point in the middle of the pattern board and back off to forty yards. With no conscious aiming, throw the gun to your shoulder and fire at the aim point. Try not to even look at the pattern yet. Do this at least a half dozen times. Now note how closely the aiming point is to the center of the multi-shot pattern. If the aim point is significantly off center that explains why you can't hit a bull in the caboose with your shotgun.

It's possible the barrel may be bent. This is more common in guns with a single barrel than double barrels. Of course, a major bend is readily visible but it doesn't take much of a kink to throw

Many shotguns do not shoot where they are pointed. Fire multiple shots at an aiming point on a pattern board to see if the pattern is off center.

the pattern way off forty yards downrange. Use a long straight-edge to check the barrel all the way around. The straightedge won't lay perfectly along the barrel because of the barrel contour but you should be able to tell if the gap between the barrel and straightedge is equal all the way around.

Minor bends can usually be straightened quite easily. Place the barrel bent-side up on a sturdy bench with a block of wood under each end to elevate it slightly above the bench top. Place a large "C" clamp at the middle of the bend. To distribute the clamp pressure over a longer area put a fairly stout piece of hard-wood, say about one-and-a-half inches thick and four inches long, between the clamp and barrel. Slowly tighten the clamp until you see the barrel spring just a little bit. Remove the clamp and check the bend. Continue doing this, gradually tightening the clamp a little more each time until the barrel is straightened.

It's much more likely that the off-shooting is caused by im-proper stock fit. With a shotgun your eyes are essentially the rear sight so they must be in just the right position for the gun to be properly sighted in. Three stock dimensions determine the sight picture you will see: drop at comb, cast, and pitch. We won't go into all the technicalities of accurately measuring these dimen-sions; we'll just discuss how they relate to our shooting. Think of the sight base as being where your cheek rests on the comb. If the comb is raised (less drop) it's like raising the rear sight which will make you shoot higher. If the comb is lowered (more drop), you'll shoot lower. If the comb is moved to the right (cast off), you'll shoot further to the right. If it's moved to the left (cast on), you'll shoot further to the left. Pitch is the angle of the butt in relation to a line parallel with the bore. The butt is not ninety degrees from this line, but rather some greater angle. Hold the gun up with the butt presssed flat against a wall. Note that the barrel slants downward. The more the pitch of the butt increases

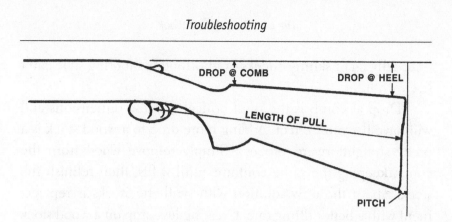

Correct stock fit is essential to accurate shotgun shooting. These are the most critical dimensions.

the further downward the barrel will point and vice versa. The same applies when your shoulder replaces the wall.

With your eyes closed, throw the gun to your shoulder just as you would when shooting. Open your eyes and look down the barrel. Do this several dozen times. You should see just the back of the receiver with the front bead stacked neatly on top or perhaps just a teeny bit of the muzzle. If the shotgun has a middle bead it should be just under the front bead to form a figure eight. If all you see is a big gob of the back of the receiver with no sign of the front bead the stock has too much drop at the comb, too much pitch, or both. On the other hand, if you see the top of the receiver and a whole bunch of barrel there is not enough drop at the comb, not enough pitch, or both.

Now place a small aim point on a wall a short distance away. Quickly shoulder the gun as if shooting at this aim point. Note the sight picture, closing the off eye if need be. If the gun is aimed directly at the target cast is okay. If it is aimed off to the left some cast off is in order. If it is aimed to the right it needs some cast on. Again, repeat this several dozen times to be sure. Most folks are fine with no cast either way but a few with unusually fat or skinny cheeks or unorthodox shooting style can't live without it.

Drop at comb is the most critical of these dimensions and will have the most effect. Adding more drop to a wood stock is a pretty straightforward process. Simply remove wood from the comb, keeping the same contours until it fits, then refinish the stock. About the only solution with synthetic stocks is replacement with a better fitting one. Creating less drop on a wood stock is another story. Gluing a hunk of wood to the top of the comb is much harder than it sounds and would look atrocious no matter how artfully done. Lace-on or adhesive-backed leather pads are available or, if you don't care about looks, simply apply layers of moleskin to the comb. If you have a showpiece stock and can't stand the thought of making it ugly, a good stock man can cut it off at the wrist and glue it back together at a different angle using a tenon joint. The joint can be well disguised with checkering. With synthetic stocks the comb can be raised with auto body filler, smoothed to shape and the stock repainted. This will add a bunch of weight, though, which affects balance. A final option is to have a gunsmith install an adjustable comb as seen on some competition guns. This allows the comb to be moved up, down, right, or left with the turn of a wrench. It's fairly expensive so bring your checkbook.

We've already touched on shotgun-slug accuracy when talking about realistic expectations. The most critical thing is using saboted slugs only in rifled barrels and Foster-style (standard shotgun slugs) in smoothbores. Every slug gun I've seen, smoothbore or rifled, has a definite ammo-brand preference. There's no rhyme or reason to it but almost always there's some make and model of slug out there that will shoot groups nearly half the size of all the others. Finding that magic bullet (well, slug) is strictly a process of trial and error.

One place where I've seen a lot of disappointment is when someone buys a rifled barrel for their pump or semi-auto bird gun expecting to turn it into a tack-driving wonder and it does little better than his old smoothbore barrel. With many interchangeable-barrel shotguns the barrel fit is quite loose. Obviously, with the barrel flopping around in the wind, groups are not likely to be impressive.

The solution is to pin the barrel. This is done by installing a tight-fitting pin running through the top of the action and into the flange on the rear of the barrel. This is best left to your 'smitty because the pin should be tapered to keep it from working down into the action, which takes some tricky fitting. Another slick way to anchor the barrel is to locate one of the scope-mount screws so

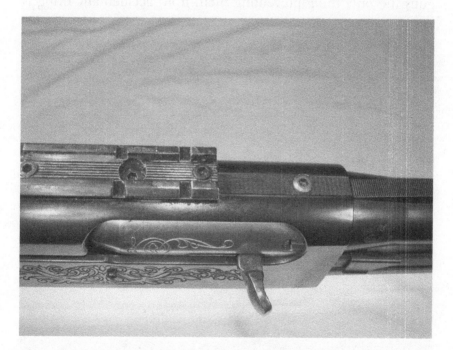

Removable shotgun barrels often fit loosely which hampers slug accuracy. Securing the barrel of this Remington 1100 with screws (two of the three screws being lengthened scope-mount screws) cut group size in half.

it threads into the barrel flange, serving the same function as the pin. The normal 6-48 base screw is too wimpy for this so alter the job to use at least an 8-32 screw, with 10-32 better yet. Just this alone took my wife's 1100 Remington smoothbore from eight-inch one-hundred-yard groups down to under four inches.

TRIGGERS

Much to-do is made over a smooth, crisp, light trigger pull and rightly so. It's impossible to shoot accurately if you have to superman-squeeze the trigger or it feels like it's full of sand. The problem is, mucking around with the trigger mechanism is very tricky. Making the slightest wrong step, even turning screws in the wrong order, can create very dangerous conditions. With most guns the only thing preventing them from accidentally firing is

The pull of simple military-style triggers can be smoothed and creep reduced by a gunsmith skilled in trigger work. It's not a job for the hobbyist.

friction contact between two little parts. The only way to smooth and lighten the trigger pull is to reduce the friction between these parts and/or lessen the contact area. The farther you go in that direction the more chance the gun is going to go bang at the most inappropriate time. *Do not attempt any trigger work yourself.*

Even adjusting adjustable triggers must be left to a knowledgeable professional. For instance, there are three trigger adjustment screws on a Remington 700. If these are adjusted in the wrong order the gun may fire when the safety is clicked off or the bolt handle moved. As I mentioned in an earlier chapter, I've personally seen this happen several times, on one occasion with blood being spilled. And Remington doesn't have a corner on that anomaly, either.

Amateurs should not attempt any trigger work. Improper adjustment of an adjustable trigger can cause accidental discharge.

You've probably guessed by now that I'm not going to delve into trigger work. I will, however, give you some trigger-pull guidelines so you don't try to talk your 'smitty into doing something he shouldn't. For a field gun that is dragged around in the brush and subject to being dropped I would not want the trigger pull less than four pounds. If you doubt this wisdom take a gun, *unloaded please,* with a trigger pull of three pounds and smack the butt sharply on the floor. As often as not the firing pin will drop. For target guns that are fired under highly controlled range conditions a two-and-three-quarter- or three-pound pull is common, but always have in mind it's a snake poised to bite.

A gunsmith accomplished in trigger work can clean up a poor trigger pull to a degree but in many cases the trigger design just doesn't lend itself to a great pull. Rather than trying to salvage the original trigger it may be preferable to replace it. A

Often the best cure for trigger ills is replacement with an aftermarket trigger unit such as this Timney Deluxe. Gunsmith installation is usually required.

number of companies such as Canjar and Timney make high-quality replacement trigger units for many of the more common rifles. Custom triggers are also available for many shotguns. Replacement triggers usually require a gunsmith to install.

SCREW REPAIR

Though it's an unforgivable sin, damaged screw slots from using the wrong-sized screwdriver is so common it's almost the norm. Minor damage is mostly just an eyesore. A severely damaged slot, though, may hinder screw tightening and removal and will only get worse. If the damage is minor it can often be repaired with a hammer and pin punch. Clamp the screw in a vise with leather padding to protect the threads. Direct the punch to peen the deformed metal back into position with light hammer taps. If needed, clean up the slot with a screw-slot file. This is a thin flat

Screw slots with minor damage can usually be cleaned up with a screw-slot file available from gunsmith-supply firms. These only have cutting teeth on the edges and come in several widths.

file with teeth only on the edges. Brownell's carries a variety of sizes to match any common screw slot width. Shape and smooth the screw head with file and sandpaper and color it with cold blue. If the damage is more severe the screw will have to be replaced.

Stripped threads is another common screw malady. If the damage is minimal the threads may be able to be restored by re-cutting them with a tap or die. Rarely are both the screw and screw-hole threads damaged, it's usually one or the other. Hardware stores carry some taps and dies but for some reason the gun industry often uses weird thread sizes. Doing the job yourself may require ordering special taps and dies from a gunsmith-supply firm. If so, you're money and grief ahead to turn the job over to a gunsmith who already has these tools.

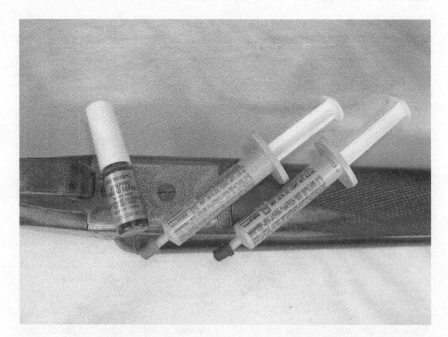

If they are not subject to too much stress, screws with stripped threads can often be made functional with an epoxy-like thread-restoring compound found at automotive stores.

If the stripped screw is not subject to a lot of stress, repair can be made with a special epoxy-type thread restorer. You can usually find this at automotive or hardware stores. Follow the label directions for preparation and mixing. The ones I've tried set up very fast so you have to work quickly.

Stuck screws can be a major pain. This is usually caused by the threads rusting together. Apply a shot of Liquid Wrench and let it soak a few hours. Be sure the screwdriver perfectly fits the slot. To let the screw know you mean business, place the screwdriver in the slot and whack the back of the handle smartly with a hammer. Give it several raps for good measure. The shock is often enough to break the screw's grip.

If you mess with enough screws, sooner or later one is going to break off down in the hole. The remains can usually be

A tool commonly referred to as an E-Z Out removes screws broken off in the hole.

removed with a tool called an E-Z Out. Available at hardware stores, this works on the order of a screw with reverse threads. A hole is drilled in the broken screw and the E-Z Out is inserted and turned. The hardest part is drilling the hole without damaging the hole threads. If the break is even you may be able to pull it off with an electric hand drill. Otherwise it may require using a drill press. Drill the full length of the broken screw to lessen its integrity.

SCREW REPLACEMENT

Obviously, severely damaged screws need to be replaced. Unfortunately, hardware-store screws rarely match those used on guns. Every gunsmith has a coffee can full of salvaged gun screws and that's the first place to turn. If that proves fruitless, gun screws are available from suppliers such as Brownell's, Gun Parts Corporation, and, of course, the factory that made the gun if it's still with us. As a last-ditch resort a gunsmith or tool-and-die shop can make a new one but it's a fairly involved process and you'll pay a lot of bucks for a few cents worth of screw.

Chapter 16

FIELD REPAIRS

We all dream of that proverbial "hunt of a lifetime" deep into unsullied wilderness. When it finally comes about, the path in has surely been paved with thousands of your dollars and it's scary to think the success of the entire mission depends on your gun performing well. So many things can go wrong. Parts

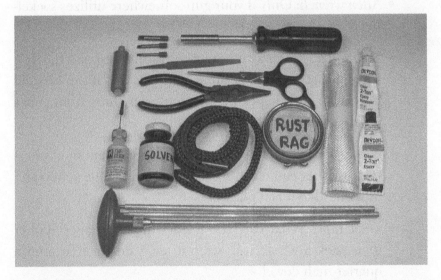

When venturing away from civilization a properly stocked repair and maintenance kit can save a hunt. Multi-blade screwdriver, allen wrench, and pliers handle disassembly chores. Epoxy, fiberglass cloth (and scissors to cut it), duct tape, and file can affect most any repair. A takedown bore-rod clears bore obstructions while the Bore Snake, solvent, lube, and rust preventive keeps your gun happy. It all fits into a Ziploc baggie.

can break, the gun could malfunction, or some mishap could cause catastrophic damage to it.

A firearm first-aid kit is essential whenever you're beyond the helping hands of a gunsmith. Whether you're traveling by bush plane, boat, horse, or boot leather, space and weight are major factors. Obviously, you need enough tools and materials to deal with emergencies without filling an entire pack. The following is a checklist of the things I take into remote areas. Most of the items also come in handy for all manner of other camp and equipment repairs.

- *Screwdriver*: The type with a single handle and inter-changeable blades is the most space efficient. Take only the blades that fit critical screws on your gun such as ac-tion screws, sight screws, and scope-ring and base screws.

- *Allen wrench*: Only if your gun somewhere utilizes socket-head screws.

- *Small file*: I prefer an automotive distributor-point file. It is small, weighs next to nothing, and cuts fast. It can be used to smooth and shape anything and everything from epoxy repairs to fingernails and fishhooks.

- *Needle-nose pliers*: I prefer these over conventional pliers because they can reach small objects inside the action and other hard-to-reach places.

- *Duct tape*: What can't be fixed with duct tape? Rather than pack a whole roll, wrap a few yards of it around a quarter-inch dowel.

- *Epoxy and fiberglass cloth*: There are few things I can think of that can't be fixed with epoxy and fiberglass, given enough ingenuity. You could lash together a broken stock, glue on a sight, mold a replacement sight blade, and even fabricate a makeshift screw. Use the long-setting version of epoxy for maximum bonding strength. Glass cloth can be obtained from boat-repair or fiberglass-mold-making shops.

- *Small scissors*: Used to cut the fiberglass cloth, first-aid tape, and other cutting chores.

- *Aluminum take-down cleaning rod*: This is more for clearing the bore of obstructions or removing a stuck casing rather than cleaning chores.

- *Bore-Snake*: For simplicity's sake I prefer this over taking brushes, patches, and jags for the rod but you can go either way.

- *Bore solvent, oil, rust preventive*: Transfer solvent and oil into small bottles holding just enough for the trip. Soak a small rag with rust preventive and store it in a Ziploc bag (test to be sure preventive doesn't dissolve bag).

- *Spare parts*: If you have the room and can afford the extra weight, a spare scope, pre-sighted for your gun, can save the trip. If you have a quality firearm decked out with quality accoutrements you shouldn't have to drag along a box of spare parts. That's precisely why you spent the big bucks to get the best to begin with. Of course, if you know your gun has a penchant for breaking or losing a certain part(s), take a spare and the tools to install it.

ADDITIONAL FOR MUZZLE LOADERS

- *Ball-pulling screw*
- *Spare nipple*

- *Nipple and drum wrenches*

- *Nipple-cleaning brush*

- *Breech-plug wrench*

You deserve all the trouble you're asking for if you run off into the boonies with a gun you're not intimately familiar with. Months prior to the great event you should shoot the gun at every opportunity to get to know its temperament and work out any bugs. Despite your best efforts, though, things can still go wrong.

Since your resources are so limited the key to effective field repair is creative thinking. If something critical breaks don't just pop the cork off a jug and drown your sorrows, figure out a way to fix it. For instance, say that old nag packhorse rolled over on your rifle and broke the stock in half at the wrist. Many a hunt has

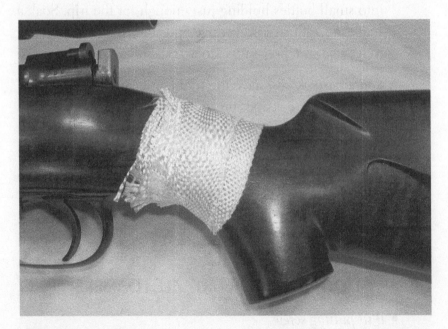

With ingenuity, fiberglass cloth and epoxy can fix most anything from a lost screw or sight to a broken stock.

abruptly ended in just such a fashion. Not yours, though. Cut long strips of fiberglass cloth to wrap around the stock wrist. Scrape away the finish from the entire wrist area with your knife to expose clean wood for the epoxy to bond to. Goober up both ends to be joined as well as the scraped area with epoxy and position the stock back together. Saturate the fiberglass strips with epoxy and tightly wrap them around the break. If need be, use small sticks and duct tape as a splint to lash everything in place until the epoxy cures. Now pop that cork to celebrate your victory. Tomorrow you can remove the duct tape, whittle off the stick splints, and smooth everything down with your emergency file. She'll feel a mite fat under your paw but you're still huntin'.

Some metal parts can be fixed in a similar manner. Epoxy (or any glue for that matter) cannot effectively bond steel, but with the addition of fiberglass cloth as a splint it just might hold the part together well enough to get through the hunt.

The epoxy-fiberglass combination can also be used to mold parts. An example would be to make a replacement rear-sight blade or front-sight bead that decided to creep out of its dovetail slot while you weren't looking. Cut small pieces of fiberglass to appropriate shape, saturate them with epoxy, work the cloth into the dovetail, and form to shape with your fingers. Keep your fingers wet to lessen the epoxy sticking to them. You'll have to keep working at it until the epoxy sets or the cloth will wander off into some other shape on its own. After the epoxy cures, shape it into final form with the file. With strips of fiberglass and epoxy you could even make such things as a scope-mount ring. I can't imagine how you'd lose one of those but stranger things have happened. Attachment screws can be molded right in. I could go on but you get the idea.

Should a critical screw break or disappear the part can likely be held in place with a fiberglass screw. Pull individual strands of glass from the cloth and cut them a bit longer than the screw. Also cut some real short strands, as short as you can make them. Use a small twig to work epoxy into the hole threads then pack the short fiberglass fibers into the threads as best you can. The epoxy itself isn't very strong but the addition of glass fibers increases strength immensely. Saturate the longer fibers with epoxy and use the twig to stuff them lengthwise into the screw hole. Again, the strength is in the fiberglass so get as many fibers in with as little epoxy as possible. Mash the ends of the strands down to form the screw head. The screw could be made stronger yet with a piece of wire or small nail formed into the middle. Worry about how you're going to get this mess back out when you get home. Smile, you're still huntin'. Stripped screw threads can be temporarily fixed with the same mixture of short glass fibers and epoxy.

The repair possibilities with epoxy and fiberglass are limitless. Strips of epoxy-saturated fiberglass can be wrapped around parts to hold them in place much stronger and firmer than duct tape. If you don't want the epoxy to bond, coat the part with gun oil or rust preventive as a release agent. Should a quick-detachable sling-swivel mechanism take a dump, bind the whole works together with fiberglass and epoxy. It's no longer quick-detachable but at least you can still sling the gun over your shoulder.

Speaking of slings, epoxy bonds very well to leather and even nylon if the weave is fully saturated. A broken sling can be repaired by saturating the ends with epoxy and overlapping them four inches or so. Use lots of epoxy and be sure it soaks into the material well.

Loss of a scope-adjustment cap exposes the delicate innards to dust and water. Cover it with a piece of plastic cut from a plastic bag, tarp, or even a candy-bar wrapper. Tie the cover on with a strand of fiberglass taken from the glass cloth. A scope-lens cover can be similarly fashioned, the upscale version being made from clear plastic wrap left over from your sandwich. If you're hunting in a monsoon, a piece of duct tape over the muzzle prevents water from getting in the bore which could act like an obstruction to elevate pressure. Tape on the outside does not affect pressure or accuracy. *Never, ever put anything inside the bore!*

Ingenuity can go a long way in devising tools, as well. Rocks and firewood serve as hammers. A nail or piece of wire works as both pin and pin punch. Shape it to fit with the file. A loop with a boot lace or section of rope twisted with a stick like a tourniquet makes a passable clamp. Our ancestors made entire civilizations with next to nothing; you can surely figure out a way to fix something well enough to get through the trip. Where there's a will there's a way if you'll unleash your brain.

INDEX

c 2013
DM 6-7-16